Parish Registers in England

THEIR HISTORY AND CONTENTS

WITH SUGGESTIONS FOR
SECURING THEIR BETTER CUSTODY AND PRESERVATION

ATTEMPTED BY

ROBT. EDMOND CHESTER WATERS, B.A.

BARRISTER OF THE INNER TEMPLE, AND
AUTHOR OF 'GENEALOGICAL MEMOIRS OF THE CHESTERS OF CHICHELEY,
THEIR ANCESTORS AND DESCENDANTS'

A NEW EDITION

REWRITTEN THROUGHOUT AND ENLARGED

Printed for the Author

LONDON
FRED. J. ROBERTS, 19 LITTLE BRITAIN, E.C.
1883

To my Friends

WILLIAM LORD EMLY AND AUBREY DE VERE

IN GRATEFUL APPRECIATION

OF THEIR GENEROUS AND CONSTANT SYMPATHY WITH

SCHOLARSHIP SUFFERING AND SORROW

This poor attempt

OF A HELPLESS AND LONELY INVALID

IN INTERVALS OF PAIN

TO DIVERT AND DISTRACT HIS THOUGHTS

IS

Affectionately Inscribed

PREFACE.

My little book on parish registers, which was reprinted with additions in 1870 from *The Home and Foreign Review* of April 1863, has long been out of print ; and on taking up the subject again after an interval of twelve years I have attempted something more than a new edition, for I have rewritten the whole from beginning to end, and my pamphlet of three sheets has grown into a book of 116 pages. It will be seen from the Preface, prefixed to my last edition and reprinted on page xi and xii, that the purpose for which my Essay was originally written is now out of date ; there is therefore no longer any reason for limiting my plan to the registers of baptism and burial, and I have recast my collections into an exhaustive history of parish registers in England from the time of their original institution in the reign of Henry VIII.

Public attention has of late been attracted to the subject by discussions arising out of the *Parish Register Preservation Bill,* which was brought into the House of Commons during the last Session. No one doubts that some statutory provision is urgently required to secure the safe custody and better preservation of the ancient registers, but it is contended by eminent antiquaries that the summary removal of the whole mass to the Record Office would operate as a serious discouragement to local research. Without presuming to determine this much-vexed question I have ventured to suggest that the problem of reconciling local and national claims is more easy of solution, than it has hitherto been supposed.

The want has long been felt of a handy and inexpensive manual of the law and practice of registration, which could be consulted with confidence and read with amusement by those, who have parish registers in their charge and take an intelligent interest in their history and contents. The only book on the subject is that of the late Mr. R. S. Burn, who was employed by the Government in the preparation of the Civil Registration Bill of 1837, and was a member of both the Royal Commissions, which were subsequently appointed for the purpose of collecting and authenticating non-parochial registers. It would be ungracious to dwell on the defects of so diligent a labourer in a newly explored field of learning, but Mr. Burn was more successful in collecting facts than in marshalling and digesting his collections, and his *History of Parish Registers* is disfigured by frequent inaccuracy of quotation, and by a want of power to grasp his subject, which makes it difficult for his readers to form a clear connected view of the different stages through which the question of registration has passed.

I am painfully conscious of my own shortcomings,

but a paralysed invalid excluded from the use of public libraries, must often be content to leave fresh clues for others to explore.

If I had good grounds twelve years ago for appealing to the indulgence of my readers in my former Preface, I have still better grounds now ; for I have been bereft in the interval of the companionship, which was my sole earthly consolation, and I have rewritten the story of parish registers under the pressure of increased infirmities. But it has been mercifully ordained that new burdens call forth fresh energies of endurance; and I have constant cause for thanksgiving in the blessing vouchsafed to me, that I have been able to continue habits of literary research during so many years of suffering.

EDMOND CHESTER WATERS.

57 THE GROVE, HAMMERSMITH :
January 1, 1883.

PREFACE TO THE EDITION OF 1870.

THIS ESSAY was originally published in the 'Home and Foreign Review,' which has long been extinct. It was written in February 1863, to serve a political as well as a literary purpose. The Government had just brought in a Bill to extend civil registration to Ireland, but to conciliate local prejudice, the marriages of the Catholic population were excluded from its provisions. This omission seemed a grievous error to those who were convinced, that a complete system of Registration without regard to religious belief had become a political necessity, and that the scruples of the Irish Catholics arose out of a misapprehension of the true objects and effect of the registration laws. The subject had hitherto attracted little attention, and it was believed that if the whole case could be brought home to the general reader, public opinion would soon insist on Catholic marriages being registered in Ireland as well as in Great Britain. This expectation was justified by the event, as will be read in the following pages.

The present Edition contains above twenty pages of new matter, and the text has been re-written throughout. The law of registration has been brought down to 1870, and the history of the English registers has been enlivened by further illustrations. The sketch is still imperfect, but it has been re-written in the intervals of pain and sickness, without access to any public library, and my materials have therefore been restricted to my own limited collections. It could never have been republished at all, but for the patience and devotion of Her, who insists on sacrificing every pleasure and pursuit in life to administer to the comfort and amusement of a hopeless and helpless invalid.

R. E. C. W.

UPTON PARK, near Poole:
    June 1870.

xiii

CONTENTS.

———•◦•———

PARISH REGISTERS.

DAVID HUME, in a well-known passage, reckons it amongst the barbarous deficiencies of the 12th century that the parish registers were irregularly kept. The truth being that parish registers were unknown in Christendom before the last decade of the 15th century.

It is more difficult, however, to excuse than to account for the anachronism. Hume and his contemporaries were better versed in ancient than in medieval learning, and scholars of this type were apt to be misled by their classical recollections in their speculations on the manners and customs of what they called the Dark Ages. A public register of births and deaths was a familiar feature of ancient civilisation, which was common to the Jews, Greeks, and Romans, from the earliest period of society with which we are historically acquainted. Hume took it for granted that the nations of medieval Europe were equally alive to the political importance of recording the growth of the population, and that registers had been adapted to the parochial system in the Middle Ages, when the duty of keeping them was transferred from the State to the parochial clergy.

The genealogical registers of the Jews were an institution of the patriarchs, which was twice renewed by Divine command in the Wilderness of Sinai before the conquest of Palestine. They formed the keystone of the Jewish theocracy, for the limitation of the Divine promises to the seed of Abraham Isaac and Jacob, the restriction of the priesthood to the descendants of Aaron, the expectation of the Messiah from the tribe of Judah and the house of David, the partition of the promised land according to tribes and families, the prohibition of intermarriage between persons of different tribes, and the perpetuity of inheritance guaranteed by the Mosaic laws, made it a religious and political necessity, as long as the Jews were a nation, that the pedigree of every Jewish family should be registered in the public archives. The registers accordingly were preserved as a sacred deposit in the Temple at

B

Jerusalem until the destruction of the city by Titus, and their authority was accepted as beyond dispute or appeal down to the latest times. After Nehemiah's return from the captivity in Babylon, the priests at Jerusalem, whose ' register was not found, were as polluted put from the priesthood : ' [1] and we know from Josephus, that the priests in his time were not permitted to marry, until they had verified from the national registers[2] the pedigrees of their intended wives.

The public registers at Sparta and Athens were as old as the constitutions of Lycurgus and Solon ; and it was a fundamental law of the Romans, which dated from the mythic reign of Servius Tullius, that when a child was born in Rome the paterfamilias paid a piece of money into the treasury of Juno Lucina. A like offering was made at the shrine of Venus Libertina whenever a kinsman died, so that the precise number of births and deaths in the city was practically ascertained from the earliest period. The register books of later times (*libri actorum*) are familiar to every reader of Ovid and Juvenal, and were the subjects of frequent legislation by the Cæsars. M. Aurelius, by a famous edict, required all free persons to deliver into the imperial treasury an account of their children within thirty days after their birth, to be registered amongst the public acts in the temple of Saturn.[3] The official lists of births and deaths, marriages and divorces, occupied a prominent place in the *acta diurna* of the empire : and registration was minutely prescribed and provided for by the code of Theodosius and the Pandects of Justinian. The ruined columns of the temple of Saturn in the Roman forum still engage the admiration of travellers, but in the 12th century the stately fabric of the Registry of imperial Rome was still standing[4] entire, although it was degraded to meaner uses by the anarchy of the papal city. A scholar therefore may be forgiven for believing that, in the age of Irnerius, Gratian, and Glanville, when Roman jurisprudence was eagerly studied in universities and blindly reverenced in courts of law, an institution of such obvious utility as the public registers would be revived or retained by the nations of Europe.

I suspect also that Hume had heard of the monastic registers, and had formed a wrong impression of their contents. In every religious house a register was kept and an obituary, as well as a chronicle. But the monastic register was a mere chartulary,

---

[1] Neh. vii. 64.
[2] *Josephus against Apion*, Book I. s. 7.
[3] Lieberkühn *de Diurnis Romanorum Actis*, Weimar, 1840.
[4] Poggius *de Variet. Fortunæ*, p. 12.

or transcript of the title deeds of possessions and privileges.[1]
Grants of founders and benefactors, royal and papal charters
of confirmation, bulls of exemption from episcopal jurisdiction,
licenses to hold lands in mortmain, final concords in the king's
court, surveys, purchase deeds and leases were copied into the
register with minute and tedious accuracy; but the laity are only
mentioned incidentally—the great in the record of their dona-
tions, and the tenants in the enumeration of their services and
rents. Nor did the obituary or chronicle supply the omissions
of the register. The obituary[2] was a list of those for whose
souls' repose the brethren were bound to offer the holy sacrifice
on their respective anniversaries: but only members of the
order, royal and ecclesiastical personages, founders, patrons, and
benefactors were commemorated by name in the precatory roll;
the rest of the faithful dead were prayed for under the vague
term of 'all Christian souls.' The chronicle contained the
annals of the house, in which the story of the foundation, the
genealogy of the founder, the progress of the fabric, the succession of abbots, and the entertainment of royal and illustrious
visitors are interspersed with details of public and local events.
But the domestic history of laymen was a subject beneath[3] the
notice of the chronicler; and if he vouchsafed to mention the
few nobles who were married or buried within the precincts,
the numerous vassals, who fought under the banner of the
abbey and peopled the demesne, married and died without a
word of record. Nor were there any parochial records; for the
secular clergy were under no obligation to keep registers, and the
parish priest found ample room in the margin of his missal and
psalter to note the few events, which he cared to record. The
obits of local magnates and the anniversaries of benefactors
were duly enrolled in the calendar prefixed to the parish missal,

---

[1] A good idea of the contents of a monastic register may be gathered from
the index of the registers of Winchcombe Abbey, printed in the *Collectanea
Topogr. and Gen.* vol. ii. pp. 16-37.

[2] Bede (*Op. Min.* p. 47) calls the obituary of Lindisfarne *the Album*; a word
which in later Latin signified 'a list of names.' (Cf. Tac. *Ann.* iv. 42.) The
obituary of the church of Durham is preserved among the Cotton MSS., and is
entitled *Liber Vitæ* from the allusions in scripture to *the Book of Life.* (Phil.
iv. 3, Rev. iii. 5.) This MS. is the finest extant example of its kind, and is
written in alternate lines of gold and silver letters, commencing from the 9th
century. It was printed by the Surtees Society in 1841.

[3] This is true of the chronicles of the greater abbeys, which alone have been
preserved; but the smaller houses, which were more dependent on fees, evidently
kept fuller records of local events than has hitherto been suspected. This
appears from the formal proofs of the heir attaining his majority (*probationes
ætatis*), in which the abbot or prior of some neighbouring house is frequently a
witness, when he usually appeals to the annals or memoranda kept by his convent,
in proof of the accuracy of his evidence.

but the great mass of Englishmen were, with literal propriety, described in the offices of the Church as ' the forgotten dead.'

It was not until the year 1497, a year famous in the annals of the world for the discovery of Newfoundland by John and Sebastian Cabot, that parochial registers in our sense of the word, embracing the whole population gentle and simple, were commenced in Europe; and they owe their introduction to the wisdom of Cardinal Ximenes. That great reformer signalised his administration of the diocese of Toledo by vigorous measures to correct the prevailing laxity of morals. At that period divorces were scandalously frequent, on the score of some pretended spiritual relationship or affinity, arising out of the act of sponsorship. Godfathers and godmothers were regarded by the Church as spiritual parents, who, with their husbands and wives and children, were spiritually related to each other and to the infant of whom they were sponsors, within the prohibited degrees. When therefore two persons wished to dissolve the bond of marriage, they had only to allege that they had previously contracted some spiritual relationship which rendered their marriage canonically invalid; and, from the absence of any record to test the truth of the allegation, they were, by an easy collusion, enabled to separate and marry some one else.[1] To remedy this abuse, the cardinal directed that an accurate register should thenceforth be kept in every parish, recording the names of the infants baptized and of their sponsors. The Archbishop of Toledo was then, with the single exception of the Holy See, the greatest ecclesiastical dignity in Christendom; and a regulation so useful to discipline, which was recommended by so high an authority, was readily accepted in other dioceses, and soon became coextensive with the Church. But for years after this date the only baptismal register at Florence, the Athens of the Middle Ages, was ludicrously primitive. The Baptistery of San Giovanni, already glorious with the gates of Ghiberti, which Michael Angelo pronounced worthy to be the gates of Paradise, was then (as in our own day) the only place in which the infants of the Florentines were baptized;

---

[1] Divorces of this kind were common in England in the 15th century, and the Records of the Church of Rochester supply many examples. The marriage between John Trevennock and Joan Peckham was dissolved on January 7, 1465, on the ground that John's former wife Letitia had been godmother to one of Joan's children; and William Lovelesse, of Kingsdown, was cited on December 29, 1472, on a charge of having married his spiritual sister; that is, a woman to whom his mother had been godmother. Offences of this kind were severely punished by the diocesan, and John Howthon, of Tunbridge, was sentenced in 1463 to be whipped three times round the market and church for marrying Dionysia Thomas, who was the goddaughter of his former wife.—Thorpe's *Customale Roffense.*

and the parish priest had no better way of calculating their numbers, than by putting beans into a bag[1]; a white bean for a girl, and a black bean for a boy; and counting the number of beans of each colour at the end of the year.[2]

In England, parish registers were unknown until the reign of Henry VIII., when the duty of keeping them was imposed on the parochial clergy by a royal injunction, which was published by Cromwell, the Vicar-General, on September 29, 1538. But although their institution was contemporary with the change of religion, and was resented as a grievance by the opponents of the new doctrines, it is a mistake to suppose that registers were of Protestant origin. Cromwell had in early life resided in the Low Countries, and was familiar with the baptismal registers introduced there by the Spanish clergy. The same shrewdness, which recognised their political value, suggested the advantage of extending them to marriages and burials when he established the system in England. He deserves the full credit of this improvement; for the ordinance of Villars Cotterets, which established registers in France in 1539, required the curé to keep nothing more than a register of *Les preuves de Baptême.*[3] The importance, however, of registering marriages as well as baptisms was soon recognised by Protestants and Catholics alike, and both registers were prescribed as a law of the Catholic Church by the Council of Trent on November 11, 1563.

Cromwell's injunction must have been projected and announced during the first year of his administration; for he was appointed the vicegerent of the king's highness, the supreme head of the Church of England, in July 1535,[4] and in 1536 the project was already exciting great discontent among the people. A rumour was widely spread that some new tax on the offices of the Church was in contemplation: and it stands first in the list of popular grievances circulated by the Insurgents of the Pilgrimage of Grace, 'That no infant shall receive the blessed sacrament of baptism onlesse an trybette be payd to the king.' Cromwell received the news of the popular discontent with his usual wariness and resolution. A minister, who had the audacity to reform the faith and observances of Catholic Christendom, was not likely to relinquish a favourite project

---

[1] Guicciardini.

[2] It is worth recording that the average annual number of baptisms at Florence from 1470 to 1494 was 2,094, and from 1794 to 1803 was 3,756; that in 1835 the number was 3,750, and that the proportion of the females to males was 113 to 100.—Murray's *Handbook of North Italy.*

[3] *Le Livre des Singularités,* 8vo, 1841, p. 312.

[4] His commission is printed in Wilkins' *Concilia,* vol. iii. p. 784.

out of deference to the scruples and ignorance of a rebellious
peasantry; but he was too prudent to strengthen the hands of
the king's enemies in a year of rebellion, and the injunctions of
1536 contain no formal order on the subject of registers.   He
had intended by establishing registers in every parish to remedy
the inconvenience to the public which was threatened by the
suppression of the smaller monasteries; and it is evident that
some instructions were given at the time of their dissolution,
for the registers of St. James, Garlickhithe, and of St. Mary
Bothaw, London, begin in November 1536, and six other
registers have been discovered of earlier date than 1538.[1]   The
increased strength of the Government and the ill success of
every attempt to oppose it, encouraged Cromwell, two years
afterwards, to resume an intention which he had never aban-
doned; and on September 29, 1538, he issued an injunction[2]
that

'The curate of every parish church shall keep one book or
register, which book he shall every Sunday take forth, and in the
presence of the churchwardens, or one of them, write and record in
the same all the weddings, christ'nings, and burials made the whole
week before; and for every time that the same shall be omitted,
shall forfeit to the said church iij*s.* iiij*d.*' &c.

In compliance with this injunction, many registers were immediately commenced; and of the extant registers which have
survived the negligence of their legal guardians in a century
incurioso suorum, no less than 812 begin from 1538.

That of St. Alkmond's, Derby,[3] begins as follows:—

'In ye 30th yeare of ye reign of King Henry 8th, in ye month
of September, Thomas Cromwell, Lord Privy Seal, Vicegerente
to ye King's Royal Highness, sent his injunction to all Bishops
& Curates through the Realme, charging them to God that in
every parish church the Bible of ye largest volume should be
placed for all men to reade on: And that a Book of Register
should be also provided and kept in every parish church, wherein
should be written every wedding, christening, and burying within
ye same Parish for ever; in obedience to which this Booke was
provided 9 November, 1538.'

The purchase of the register book is often recorded, and
the churchwarden's accounts of St. Margaret's, Westminster,
contain this entry:—

'1538. Paid for a book to registre in the names of buryals,
weddings, and christ'nings, 2*d.*'

---

[1] *London and Middlesex Archæologia,* vol. iii. part x.
[2] Burnet's *Hist. of the Reformation,* Appendix, vol. i. p. 178.
[3] *Journal Archæol. Association,* No. XXVII.

The new institution was received by the people with general alarm and mistrust, which was aggravated sometimes by the language of the register, when the vicar and churchwardens took occasion to exult in a fresh departure from the old religion.

NEWBOTTLE, NORTHAMPTONSHIRE. '1538, Oct. 1. Thys Boke, mayde by ye expresse comandement of our most Sovereygne Lorde Kynge Henry VIII., by ye grace of Gode Kynge of Englande and of France, Defender of ye feyth, Lord of Yreland, and ye supreme hede in earth of this hys church of England, for certen goodly usys, by hys ryght excellent wyse and sage Counsail, divised and upon lyke consideracons instituted as by the divisyons of ye same, in iij sondrie places here folowynge may apere, begynnynge in ye yere of hys prosperous and honorable reyne xxx, and in ye yere of our mayster Christ, M.D,XXX,VIIJ, fyrst day of October, to be exercysed after ye forme as therafter ensueth. The Lord Thos. Crumwell, Lord privyseale and vicegerent to hys hyghnese of ye ecclesiastycal jurisdiction, exhibiting to us of ye clergye ye same w^t dyverse other at ye time lyke fruytful and laudable inventions, meted to ye glorye of God, to the Kynges honour, and to ye great benefyts of ye hys realme, and annihilatynge of ye bysshop of Rome hys long falsly pretensyd and usurped powres. I, Edward Medley, beynge Vicar here, Robert Wyat and Thomas Harden, Churchwardens, statyng our lyke assyduouse prayer w^t all fidelyte and obsequence to ye accomplesshmet of ye contentes of ye same. 'Amen.'[1]

The state of public feeling in the West of England is described by Sir Piers Edgcumb in a contemporary letter[2] to Cromwell, which strikingly illustrates the watchfulness of the Government in that reign of innovation and severity. The letter is written in the knight's own hand, and runs thus :—

'SIR PIERS EGGECUME TO CRUMWELL.

' Please it, ywr goode Lordeshyp to be advertyssed, that the Kyngg's Majesty hath commandyd me, at my beynge in hys gracius presens, that in casse I parcyvyd any grugge, or miscontentacyon among his sojectes, I shulde ther off advertysse ywr Lordeshyp by my wrytynge. Hyt ys now comme to my knolegge, this 20 daye of Aprill, by a ryght trew honest man, a servant off myn; that ther ys moche secrett and several communycacyons amongges the Kyngge's sojettes; and that off them, in sundry places with in the scheres off Cornwall and Devonsher, be in great feer and mystrust; what the Kyngges Hyghnes and hys Conseylle schulde meane, to geve in commaundement to the parsons and vycars off every parisse, that they schulde make a booke, and surely to be kept, wher in to be specyffyyd the namys off as many as be weddyd, and the namys off them that be buryyd and of all those that be crystynyd.

---

[1] Baker's *Hist. of Northamptonshire.*

[2] Burn mistakes the date of this letter, which was evidently written, April 20, 1539. Sir Piers died August 14, 1539. Burn's *Hist. of Parish Registers*, 1862, p. 9.

Now ye maye perceyve the myndes off many. What ys to be don, to avoyde ther unserteyn conjecturys, and to contynue and stablysse ther hartes in trew naturell loff, accordynge ther dewties, I refferre to ywr wyssdom. Ther mistrust ys, that somme charges, more than hath byn in tymys past, schall growe to theym by this occacyon off regesstrynge of thes thyngges; wher in, yff hyt schall please the Kyngges Majeste to put them yowte off dowte, in my poar mynde schall encresse moche harty loff. And I beseche our Lorde preserve yow ever, to Hys pleasser, 20th daye off Apryll.   Scrybelyd in hast.   P. Eggecomb.'
            (Superscribed)
    'To my Lorde Privy Seale, ys goode Lordessyhyp, be this gevyn.'

It will be observed that the injunction casts the whole duty on the clergy, and imposes neither payment nor penalty on the parishioners; but the question of fees has in every age been a difficulty inseparable from registration. Such payments were as distasteful to the deprived Catholic priests, who did not receive them, as to the laity, who had to pay them; and in 1548 the royal proclamation inhibited all persons from preaching without a license, expressly on the ground [1] that

'certain popish preachers endeavoured, in their sermons, to possess people of scandalous reports against the king, as if he intended to lay strange exactions on the people, and to demand half-a-crown apiece for every one who should be married, christened, or buried.'

New injunctions were issued from time to time in the succeeding reigns, but the ordinance of registers remained substantially unchanged until 1597. The only alteration which I have observed in the interim is, that Cardinal Pole in 1555 required the names of the godfathers and godmothers to be added in the register of baptisms, according to the practice of Italy and Spain.[2] This addition has been of obligation in Catholic countries since November 1563, when it was enjoined by the Council of Trent, but it was never the law of the Anglican church, except during the reign of Queen Mary, and Cardinal Pole's injunction was then only partially obeyed. It has never, however, been forbidden to Anglicans to record the names of the sponsors, and the custom was retained by the parish of St. Nicholas, Newcastle-on-Tyne, and probably by many others, up to the beginning of the present century.

---

[1] Fuller's *Church Hist.*, ed. Brewer, vol. iv. p. 31, and Strype's *Memorials*, vol. ii. p. 90.
[2] Hook's *Lives of Archbishops of Canterbury*, viii. 427. The sponsors are invariably mentioned in the baptismal registers of the English Catholics to this day.

On October 25, 1597, the clergy of Canterbury in convocation made a new ordinance respecting registers, which was formally approved by the queen under the great seal. It commences by noticing their very great utility (*permagnus usus*), and lays down minute regulations for their preservation, which were afterwards embodied in the 70th canon of 1603. Every minister at his institution was to subscribe to this protestation :—

'I shall keep the register-book according to the queen's majesty's instructions.'

Every parish was to provide itself with a parchment book, in which the entries from the old paper books were to be fairly and legibly transcribed, each page being authenticated by the signature of the minister and churchwardens,

'so far as the ancient books thereof can be procured, but especially since the beginning of the reign of the late queen.'

This parchment book was to be kept in a 'sure coffer with three locks,' of which the minister and each churchwarden was to keep a key; and, for further security against loss, a true copy of the names of all persons christened, married, or buried in the year before was to be transmitted every year to the bishop of the diocese, within a month after Easter, to be preserved in the episcopal archives. The 70th canon has never been repealed, and the registers were kept by the clergy, under its authority, until the passing of Rose's Act in 1812.

The oldest register-books now extant are usually transcripts made in pursuance of the injunction of 1597 or 1603, at the expense of the parish.

LEVERTON,[1] CO. LINCOLN, Churchwardens' accounts, 1599 :—

'Paid for parchement for the newe Regester booke vij*s*.

Paid for makeing and writtinge therein baptizemige, marryage, and burialls that conteyned in the old Regester booke xiij*s*. iiij*d*.'

LOUGHBOROUGH. '1601 John Dawson did copy and write out this book out of the old paper book when he was at the age of three score and one years, and at that time had been Schoolmaster of the Grammar School thirty-six years, and in his time taught and brought up many Scholars, Gentlemen, Men of Worship, Justices of Peace, and Poor Men's Sons, profitable to the Church of God, Preachers and Ministers, beneficial and comfortable to the Commonwealth, advancing greatly the Glory of God.'

In some few parishes the original paper books are still in existence; and it has been discovered from a careful collation

---

[1] *Archæologia*, vol. xli. p. 367.

with the vellum transcript, that the original entries are often abbreviated in the copy. For example,[1]

ST. DUNSTAN'S WEST. '1560-1, Feb. 17. Mr. Rithe buried.'

The old paper book adds,

'a benchar of Lyncolnes Yne, buryed out of the newe brycke byldynge, beynge in owre p'ishe, the hether syde of Lyncolnes Yne.'

The growth of Protestant sentiment in the interval between 1538 and 1597, is illustrated by the transcriber's omission of prayers and pious supplications for the souls of the dead.

STAPLEHURST, KENT. When the register was recopied, the words printed between brackets were left out of the transcript.

'1543. Dec. 31. There was buried John Turner the elder [whose sowle Jesu pardon. Amen].

'1545. June 6. buryed the sonn of Thomas Roberts the younger, called Henry [upon whose soule I pray God have mercy].

'1548. Sept. 11. buryed James Bragelond an honest man and a good householder [whose soule Jesu pardon, and bring to eternal rest].'

In obedience to the injunction every page of the transcript is signed by the minister and churchwardens of that year in which the copy was made. This circumstance gave rise to a ludicrous notion respecting the longevity of the clergy of the sixteenth century, which at one time found strenuous defenders amongst antiquarian writers.[2] Duncomb,[3] in his *History of Herefordshire*, gravely asserts,

'Robert Barnes was vicar of Bromyard eighty-two years, as his name appears during the whole of that period in the parochial registers, and one of his churchwardens filled that office from 1538 to 1600.'

Gorham attributes equal longevity to the Vicar of St.[4] Neots, and the Historian of Leicestershire assures us that the Vicar of Keyham held his living ninety-two years, and had the same churchwardens for seventy years.[5]

The canons of 1603 were made by the bishops and clergy in convocation, convened by the king's writ, and were afterwards confirmed by the king under the great seal; but it was decided by the Court of King's Bench, in a celebrated judgment,[6] that although they were clearly binding on the clergy they did not *proprio vigore* bind the laity. Bearing this in mind, it is remarkable that no part of the canon has been so badly observed, as the duty imposed on the bishops. It

[1] *Coll. Top. and Gen.* vol. iv. p. 116-18.   [2] Cole's *MSS.* xli. 310.
[3] Duncomb's *Hist. of Co. Hereford*, vol. ii. p. 83.   [4] Gorham's *Hist. of St. Neots.*
[5] Nichols's *Hist. of Leicestershire*, vol. iii., p. 980.   [6] Middleton v. Crofts.

had been wisely ordered that a correct transcript should yearly
be sent to the bishop of the diocese; and the utility of this
provision in supplying local loss, and preventing the commission of fraud, has been signally proved in parliamentary [1] and
legal proceedings; but the canon attached no fees to the transcript either for the parish or the bishop, and neither of them
was zealous of employment without remuneration. The result
has been that the parishes often grudged the expense of a copy,
the bishops seldom insisted on its transmission, and the diocesan registrars allowed their archives to remain 'unarranged
and unconsultable;'[2] so that the bishops' transcripts, which
ought to have formed an invaluable department of the public
records, present a lamentable picture of episcopal negligence
parochial parsimony and official rapacity.[3]

During the civil war, parish registers shared in the general
confusion of the Anglican Church, and were for the first time
regulated by Act of Parliament. On December 6, 1644, the
subject was specially referred by the House of Commons to
the Committee, who had in charge the Directory for the public
worship of God; and on January 3, 1644–5, a few days before
the execution of Archbishop Laud, the Directory was by a
solemn ordinance[4] substituted for the Book of Common Prayer.
The Directory ordained that 'a fair register-book of velim'
should be provided in every parish, and that the names of all
children baptized, and the time of their birth, and also the
names of all persons married and buried, should be set down
therein by the minister. It should be remarked that this is
the first instance of the minister being required to register
births as well as baptisms.

The registers of this period abound with curious notices
of the ecclesiastical anarchy which then prevailed. Thus:—

ROTHERBY, CO. LEICESTER. '1643, Bellum! 1644, Bellum! 1645,
Bellum! interruption! persecution! . . . . . Sequestration by

---

[1] Chandos Peerage case, Leigh Peerage case, &c.

[2] Evidence of Sir William Betham before the Committee in 1832.

[3] Lest I should be accused of exaggeration, I will state a few facts from
the Report on the Public Records of 1800. The diocese of Winchester includes
142 parishes in Surrey, and the Registry only has twenty registers for all these
parishes from 1597 to 1800. As every parish ought to have annually sent a copy
of its register, for 203 years, there is here a deficiency of 28,206 registers.
Salisbury contains 434 parishes: only 9 or 10 were in the habit of sending copies
in 1800: in Rochester, 7 parishes, out of 95, sent transcripts in 1800. The
Registrar of London coolly certified to the commissioners: 'I hereby certify
that *it is not the custom* within the diocese of London for any return to be made
to the Bishop's Registry of either burials or baptisms.' Mr. Bruce found, in
1848, that at Lincoln the parchment transcripts were regularly cut up by the
registrar for binding modern wills.

[4] *Parliamentary Hist. of England,* vol. iii. p. 322.

John Mussen, yeoman, and John Yates, taylor! 1649, 1650, 1651, 1652, 1653, 1654, Sequestration ! Thomas Silverwood, intruder.'

KIBWORTH, CO. LEICESTER. ' Ano Dni 1641. Know all men, that the reason why little or nothing is registered from this year 1641 until the year 1649, was the civil wars between King Charles and his Parliament, which put all into a confusion till then; and neither minister nor people could quietly stay at home for one party or the other.'

ST. MARY'S, BEVERLEY. 1643, June 30. ' Our great scrimage in Beverley, and God gave us the victory at that tyme, ever blessed be God.'

1643, July 30. 'Thirteen slaine men on yᵉ King's party was buried.'

> 'All our lives now at yᵉ stake,
> Lord deliver us, for Christ his sake.'

ST. BRIDGET'S, CHESTER. ' 1643. Here the Register is defective till 1653. *The tymes were such.*'

HILTON, DORSET. ' 1649. At my first coming to this place, about this time, there war som married that livid in the parish, others buried, and especially more that had their children baptized, partly in contempt, and by reason of ignorance and wilfulness against me refusing to be examined, of the poorer sort, and whereof som ar living, others ar dead, the which if they should live, they would be made uncapable of any earthly inheritance (this I note for the satisfaction of any that do) And so I left it in the clarks liberty.—WILLIAM SNOKE, *Minister.*'

MAID'S MORETON, BUCKS. 'A.D. 1642. This year the worst of Parliaments wickedly rebelling against the best of Princes King Charles I.; the kingdom underwent most sad affliction, especially churches, whilst they pretended reformation, were everywhere robbed and ruined by the Rebells. In this Church of Moreton the windows were broken, a costly desk in the form of a spread eagle gilt, on which we used to lay Bp. Jewel's works, doomed to perish as an abominable Idoll; the Cross (which, with its fall, had like to have broke out the brains of him that did it) cut off the steeple by the soldiers at the command of one called Colonel Purefoy of Warwickshire. He carried away what he could, and, among other things, the Register was hid; and for that cause is not absolutely perfect for divers years, tho' I have used my best diligence to record as many particulars as I could come by.

'A.D. 1653. Now came in force a goodly act made by the usurper Cromwell's little Parliament, or the Parliament of Saints, as they called it, that is, of all manner of dissembling hypocrites and filthy hereticks, who ordered not the baptism, but the birth of children to be recorded in the parish Register, thereby insinuating that children ought not to be baptized, and encouraging people to withhold their infants from the sacred ordinance. But there were never any that I knew of that mind in Moreton. And though the baptism of some be not expressed here, yet they are to certify all whom it may concern, and that on the word of a Priest, that there is no person hereafter mentioned by the then registers of the parish, but was duly and orderly baptized.

'By the Act before mentioned in the year 1653 marriages were not to be performed by the Minister, but the Justices of the Peace, yet none in this parish were bedded before they were solemnly wedded, in the Church, and that according to the orders of the Church of England.'[1]

It will be gathered from these extracts that the system of leaving parochial registration to the clergy broke down during the Commonwealth; but the evil was recognised, and a remedy provided by that eminent Committee for the reformation of the law, on which Whitelocke, Sydney, and Shaftesbury were associated with the ablest lawyers of the Long Parliament. Of all the questions which engaged the consideration of the Committee, the reconstruction of the marriage laws was the most urgent and popular. The common law of England regarded marriage as a religious contract, which fell within the exclusive jurisdiction of the Church, and the duties of celebrating and registering marriages were strictly reserved to the clergy. The abolition of the Bishops' Courts, which had the sole cognisance of matrimonial causes, made legislation imperative; and the Independents, who were then the dominant party, were bent on divesting marriage of its religious character, and on transferring the whole jurisdiction from the clergy to the civil magistrate. The Committee accordingly prepared a bill to adjust the law to the altered relations between Church and State, and the requirements of public opinion. But although their deliberations were wise, their action was slow,[2] and exhausted the patience of the nation; and when the Long Parliament was forcibly dispersed by Cromwell in April 1653, their projects of legal reform were still only in draft waiting for legislation. Marriage and Registration, however, were subjects of too much general interest to be allowed to drop; and on the following 24th of August the draft bill of the Committee was, with a few verbal alterations, made law by PraiseGod Barebones' Parliament.[3] By this Act, the clergy were required to give up their register-books to laymen, who were to be called the 'parish registers.'

These new officials were to enter fairly in the books in their keeping all publications of banns, marriages, births, and burials, with the dates thereof and the names of the parties, and were empowered to charge a fee of 12*d.* for every certificate of pub-

---

[1] Lipscombe's *Hist. of Bucks*, vol. iii. p. 47.
[2] Ludlow's *Memoirs*, 4to, 1771, pp. 175, 184.
[3] *Parl. Hist. of England*, vol. iii. p. 1413, and Scobell's *Acts during the Commonwealth*, fol. 1658.

lication and entry of marriage, and of 4*d.* for every entry of birth and burial. The Act does not mention baptisms, and therefore, in most parishes, births only were recorded at this period. The lay register was to be chosen in every parish by the inhabitant householders on or before September 22, 1653, and as soon as he had been sworn and approved by the local magistrate, his appointment was to be entered in the register-books. Thus :—

AYLESBURY, BUCKS.[1] 'John Jordan, of Aylesbury, in the county of Bucks clerke, being by the major part of the parish of Aylesbury, present at the church uppon the 20th day of Sept. in the year 1653, chosen Register, according to an Act of Parliament entitled, An Act touching Marriages and the Registry thereof, as also touching Birth and Burials, dated the 24th of August 1653 : we therefore, whose names are under-written, Justices of the Peace for the said County, doe approve of the said John Jordan to be Register, and to have the keeping of the register booke for the said parish of Aylesbury, under our hands this 20 Sept. 1653.'

'WILLM. ABELL. HENRY PHILLIPS. RICHD. DALBY.'

ELWICK, CO. DURHAM. 'Maryinge by justices, *election of registers* by parishioners, and the use of ruling elders, first came into fashion in the time of rebellion, under that monster of nature and *bludy* tyrant, Oliver Cromwell.'

ISELHAM, CAMBS. '1653–4, Feb. 11. Edmund Shilling took the oaths, being chosen to be *Presbyter.*

'1658. Edmund Shilling, parish clerk and *sworn Register,* buried 2 May.'

.The statutory designation of the 'Register' was not a new title coined for the purpose of this Act, for Archbishop Cranmer's nephew, who had charge of the Registry of the Archdeacon of Canterbury in the reign of Queen Elizabeth, is thus described in the burial register of St. Mildred's, Canterbury :—

'1604, June 5. Mr. Thomas Cranmer, *Register.*'

Such officials are now commonly styled *Registrars,* but this is a solecism of modern invention, and no such word as Registrar will be found in the older statutes, or in Johnson's *Dictionary.* In the language of Roman jurisprudence,[2] the archivist was *regerendarius,* and the archives were *regesta,*

---

[1] Lipscombe's *Hist. of Bucks.* vol. ii. p. 56.
[2] Prudentius, Peristeph. x. 1131.

> Hic in *regestis* est liber cælestibus,
> Monumenta servans laudis indelebilis.

Fl. Vopiscus in the Life of Probus, 'Usus sum *regestis* scribarum.' Regestum and regerendarius both occur in the Codes ; see Cujacius, xv. c. 37.

from which came in low-latin *registrum* and *registrarius*. When the *registrarius* signed Latin documents officially, he subscribed himself for brevity ' *Registrar*,' just as the *Prebendarius* signed himself ' *Prebendar* '; and the abbreviation of the Latin signature came to be mistaken in a generation ignorant of Latin for the official designation in English. At Oxford, the keeper of the University archives is still styled the Register, but at Cambridge he is more consistently called the Registrary.

The Register's duties under this Act were not limited to registration, for it was now enacted that, after September 29, 1654, no marriage was to be celebrated within the Commonwealth of England without the Register's certificate that he had published banns in three ' successive Lord's days at the close of the morning Exercise in the public meeting place commonly called the church or chapel, or (if the parties preferred it) in the nearest market-place on three successive market-days.' The persons intending to be married were to take this certificate to the nearest Justice of the peace, when the man was to take the woman by the hand and pronounce plainly and distinctly the following words:

'I (A. B.) do here in the presence of God the searcher of all hearts, take thee (C. D.) for my wedded wife, and do also in the presence of God and before these witnesses promise to be unto thee a loving and faithful husband.'

Then the woman was in like form to promise to be

'a loving, faithful, and obedient wife;'

whereupon the Justice was to declare them man and wife.

It will be observed that nothing is said about the ring, which has from time immemorial been used in the marriage service; but the marriage ring was assumed to be of heathen origin, and it was gravely debated by the zealots whether it ought not to be prohibited. This did not escape ridicule after the Restoration, and we read in Hudibras:

' Others were for abolishing
This tool of matrimony, a ring,
With which th' unsanctify'd Bridegroom
Is marry'd only to a thumb
(As wise as ringing of a pig
That us'd to break up ground and dig),
The Bride to nothing but her will,
That nulls the after-marriage still.'

Another part of the marriage ceremony which shocked the Saints of the Commonwealth was the kiss, in which the officiating priest joined:

' A contract of eternal Bond of Love,
  Confirmed by mutual jointure of your hands,
  Attested by the *Holy close of Lips,*
  Strengthened by interchangement of your rings.' [1]

The Protestants, however, seem from the first not to have
relished kissing the priest, for it is one of the Articles of
Visitation in the diocese of London in 1554 :

'Whether there be any that refuseth to kysse the Prieste
at the solempnisation of matrimony, or use any such lyke ceremonies heretofore used and observed in the Churche.' [2]

Up to the time of the passing of this Act a marriage by the
form prescribed in the book of Common Prayer had been valid,
although the celebrant was liable to a fine of £5 for not using
the form inserted in the Directory of Public Worship. Still many
people clung to the ancient service, and amongst others Stephen
Marshall the Preacher, who had a chief hand in compiling the
Directory, deliberately made use of the Prayer Book in marrying
his own daughter, when he paid down to the churchwardens the
legal fine which he had incurred.

It was soon found that, although zealots were gratified by
the enactment of civil marriages, it was resented by the mass
of the people as a grievance that they were not allowed to
marry in church, and therefore, when the marriage Act was
confirmed in 1656, the declaration was omitted that no other
marriage, except by a magistrate, was valid. It now became a
common practice for marriages to be celebrated by the Minister
and the Mayor of the town jointly.

St. Mary Magdalene, Launceston.   '1657–8, 5 Jan.   Were
married by Nicholas Gennis, gent. & Maior of this Towne, and
also by Mr. William Oliver, Minister of this Towne, Thomas
Roberts, the sonne of Christopher Roberts, of the p'ish of Lipton
in Devon, and Elizabeth Glanvile the daughter of Oliver Glanvile
of this Towne, gent., deseesed. Thir Banes beeing by mee published three severall Lords dayes without contradiction.'

The employment, however, of the Minister was a conces-
sion to old customs, which was rejected by the Independents as
savouring of superstition; and when the Protector's daughter
was married in the next year, it was thought politic that the
Court should set the example of a civil marriage in the
strictest form.

St. Martin's in the Fields.   '1657, Nov. 11.   These are to
certifie whom it may concerne, that according to a late Act of
Parliament, entytuled an Act touching Marriages, and the regis-

---

[1] Twelfth Night, act v. scene i.   [2] *Collectanea Top. et Geneal.* iii. 325.

tering thereof, &c. Publication was made in the publique meeting place, in the Parish Church of the Parish of Martins in the Fields in the county of Middlesex, upon three several Lord's Days, at the close of the morning exercise, namely, upon the xxv. day of October MDCLVII., as also upon the I. and VIII. day of November following, of a marriage agreed upon between the Honorable Robert Rich of Andrew's Holborn, and the Right Honorable the Lady Frances Cromwell, of Martins in the Fields, in the county of Middlesex. All which was fully performed according to the Act without exception.

'In witness whereof I have hereunto set my hand the IX. day of November, MDCLVII.

'WILLIAM WILLIAMS.

'*Register of the Parish of St. Martins in the Fields.*'

Then follows, in the hand of Henry Scobell, the clerk of the Parliaments, and a Justice for Westminster—

'Married, XI. Novemb., MDCLVII, in the presence of His Highness the Lord Protector, the Right Honble. the Earls of Warwick and Newport, Robert Lord Birch, the Lord Strickland, and many others.'

It will be observed that the authorities were so unwilling to recognise the saints in those days of civil marriages, that the parishes are studiously described as 'Martin's and Andrew's' in the Register. But it is amusing to learn from Dugdale's account of this wedding (in a letter preserved at Trentham [1]) that this overstrained godliness to meet the public eye was followed by profane merriment in private.

'1657, Nov. 14.—On Wednesday last was my Lord Protector's daughter married to the Earl of Warwick's grandson ; Mr. Scobell, as a Justice of the peace, tyed the knot after a godly prayer made by one of His Highnesses divines ; and on the Thursday was the wedding feast kept at Whitehall, where they had 48 violins and 50 trumpets, and much mirth with frolics, besides mixt dancing (a thing heretofore accounted profane) till 5 of the clock yesterday morning. Amongst the dancers there was the Earl of Newport, who danced with Her Highness.'

The legislation of the Commonwealth was ignored after the Restoration, but the inconvenience of bastardising the issue of civil marriages was so apparent, that civil marriages by justices were legalised by Act of Parliament [2] in 1660.

The experiment of civil registration was successful, for the register-books from 1653 to 1660 were kept exceptionally well ; but unfortunately they are often missing, from the clergy failing to get possession of them on resuming their livings.

[1] Letter to Sir Richard Leveson, of Trentham, Staffordshire, printed in *Fifth Report of Hist. MS. Commission*, p. 177.
[2] 12 Car. II. c. 33.

It might have been expected that the registers of the Commonwealth period would abound with Puritan names, but according to my experience such names occur more frequently at an earlier date. For example:—

St. Dunstan's West, London. '1599, April 19. *Repente*, a child of Thos. Kytchens.'

Chiddingley, Sussex.[1] '1616, Mary, wife of *Freegift* Mabbe, bur. 1618, *Restore* Weekes and *Constant* Semar, marr. 1621, John, son of *Freegift* Bishop, bapt. 1631, Thos. Perse and *Faintnot* Kennard marr.'

It is almost certain that *Praisegod* Barbone the most conspicuous member of the Parliament of 1653, received his name at his baptism, for he is so named in the books of the Leathersellers'[2] Company of London, when he took up his freedom on Jan. 20, 1623–4; but the godly names of Cromwell's saints were, for the most part, mere names of adoption. Thus Praisegod's brother styled himself '*If-Christ-had-not-died-for-thee-thou-shouldest-have-been-damned* Barbone' which was abbreviated by the profane to *Damned* Barbone; and Milcom Groat changed his baptismal name Milcom for '*The-abomination-of-the-children-of-Ammon*.' This custom became a standing subject of ridicule with the wits of the Restoration, and it will be remembered that the cutter of Coleman Street, in Cowley's play, protests

'Sister Barebottle, I must not be called Cutter any more; that is a name of Cavalero Darkness. . . . . My name is now Abednego. I had a vision which whispered to me through a keyhole, Go, call thyself Abednego.'

It is still a vexed question whether the names of the famous Sussex jury[3] were really given to them at baptism. They were named, *Accepted* Trevor, *Redeemed* Compton, *Faintnot* Hewit, *Makepeace* Heaton, *God Reward* Smart, *Standfast on High* Stringer, *Earth* Adams, *Called* Lower, *Kill Sin* Pimple, *Return* Spelman, *Be Faithful* Joiner, *Fly Debate* Roberts, *Fight the Good Fight of Faith* White, *More Fruit* Fowler, *Hope for* Bending, *Graceful* Harding, *Weep not* Billing, *Meek* Brewer.

At the Restoration the parochial clergy recovered possession of the registers, and in many cases their first act was to insert an entry expressive of their contempt and disgust for the intruding ministers, who had superseded them during the Protectorate.

---

[1] *Sussex Archæologia*, vol. xiv. p. 246.
[2] *Gent. Mag.* July 1848. Praise God Barbone was buried at St. Andrew's, Holborn, 5 Jan. 1679–80.
[3] *Parl. Hist.* vol. iii. p. 1,408, note.

GAINFORD, CO. DURHAM.[1] '1660. Sequuntur paginæ vetusti hujus matricis Ecclesiæ Sti. Cuthberti de Gainford registri, sub tempore Vicariæ Dni. Cradock (qui et Prebendar. Dunelm. et Archidiaconus Northumbriæ) conscripti quotquot Sandersoni liberorum ungues evaserunt, a patre nimirum doctorum sive a natura seu ab exemplo omnia quæcumque discerpere, et in omnia digitos rapaces injicere, a nobis vero haud minore cura et sollicita pietate quam sibillina folia collecta consarcinata et compacta.

'HENRY GRESWOULD, Vicar.'

EVERLEY, WILTS.[2] '1660. In perpetuam rei infamiam sub Stratocratia Oliveri Cromwelli, qui scelere dolo sanguine proditione tum aliorum, tum sui præsertim principis, hujus regni imperium rapuit, homuncio quidam, effrictæ frontis, Gulielmus Eastman (vulgo Tinker appellatus, occupatione vero faber ærarius) in parochiæ hujus Rectoriam ingestus erat, hinc graculus per quinquennium concionabatur, multos novatores et infimæ sortis plebeios in suam traxit dissimulationem. Carolo IIdo. restaurato expulsus est, non sine magno asseclarum suorum cordolio, Sep. 30, 1660; sed meliorum conviciis et scommatibus abunde proscissus, abiit cum pannis.

> ' Exit Tinker, let all men henceforth know
>   A thorn was planted where a vine should grow;
> Down went St. Paul, Apollos, and Cephas,
>   For silver trumpets here was sounding brass.'

Registers were kept in the ancient fashion until 1678, when a new and more stringent enactment ' for burying in woollen' required an entry to be made in the register of burials that the Act had been duly complied with. This singular sumptuary law for the dead was devised by the Parliament of 1666,[3] and was conceived in the same barbarous spirit of protection, as that which prohibited[4] the importation of cattle bred in Ireland, and of fish taken by foreigners. It was professedly passed ' for the encouragement of the woollen manufactures, and prevention of the exportation of moneys for the buying and importing of *linen*;' and it enacted that after March 25, 1667, no person should be ' buried in any shirt, shift, or sheete, other than should be made of wooll onely.' The provisions of the Act were so strict that even the quilling round the inside of the coffin, and the ligature round the feet of the corpse, were required to be of woollen. But custom is stronger than legislation, and the practice of wrapping the dead in linen is older than Christianity itself. The statute was generally disobeyed, and the penalty could seldom be enforced, because an informa-

---

[1] Surtees' *Hist. of Co. Durham*, vol. iv. p. 12.
[2] The Rev. J. E. Jackson, of Leigh, Delamere, has kindly collated this extract with the register for the purpose of correcting the blunders and misprints which disfigure the version printed in Hoare's *Modern Wiltshire*.
[3] 18 & 19 Chas. II. c. 4.   [4] *Ibid.* c. 2.

tion could only be laid by those who were most interested in concealing the offence. To remedy this, a more stringent Act was passed in 1678,[1] which obliged the clergy to make an entry in the register that an affidavit had been brought to them within eight days after the burial, certifying that the requirements of the law had been fulfilled. It now became the practice for the parish clerk to call out at the grave, immediately after the conclusion of the burial service, ' Who makes affidavit ? ' upon which one of the relations came forward and made the necessary oath, which was duly noticed in the register. The common form of affidavit is printed verbatim from a facsimile, reproduced in the *Sussex Archæologia* [2] :—

' *Elizabeth Bryant*, of the parish of *Radmill*, in the county of *Sussex*, maketh oath, that *Elizabeth Ford*, of the parish of *Radmill*, in the county of *Sussex*, lately deceased, was not put in, wrapt up, or wound up, or buried in any shirt, shift, sheet, or shroud, made or mingled with flax, hemp, silk, hair, gold, or silver, or other than what is made of sheep's wool only ; nor in any coffin lined or faced with any cloth, stuff, or any other thing whatsoever made or mingled with flax, hemp, silk, hair, gold, or silver, or any other material contrary to the late Act of Parliament for burying in woollen, but sheep's wool only. Dated the 16 day of *Jan.* 1724.'

Whilst the Act remained in force, it was usually entered in the register that the law had been complied with in the burial :

NEWBURN-ON-TYNE. ' 1687, 18 Aug. Cuthbert Longridge was buried in woollen, as by a certificate dated 24 Aug. 1687.'

LAMESLEY, CO. DURHAM. ' 1678. Anne Marley wrapped in sheep's skin, bur.'

WOOLVERCOT, OXON. ' 1693, August 17. Catherine dau. of Sir William Juxon, buried in woollen—affidavit.'

The Act of 1678 was more successful in enforcing the penalty than in changing the custom of the higher classes, who regarded it rather as a tax to be paid than a law to be observed. There are frequent proofs of this in the registers ; but it will be sufficient to quote the examples of Colonel Walter, Lieutenant-General of the Ordnance, and Mrs. Oldfield the actress.

WOOLVERCOT, CO. OXON. ' 1679, April 30. David Walter, Esquire, Lord of Godstowe, buried ; but not according to the Act of Parliament, whereupon an information being given to a justice of the peace, the executor, Sir William Walter, ordered 50*s.* to be paid to the poor of the parish, the other 50*s.* being paid to the informer.'

---

[1] 30 Chas. II. c. 3.
[2] *Sussex Archæologia*, vol. xviii. p. 192.

WESTMINSTER ABBEY. 1730. 'Mrs. Ann Oldfield was buried in the south aisle 27 Oct.'

She lies beneath the monument[1] of Congreve, and according to the testimony of her maid, Elizabeth Saunders, her body was by her express request dressed 'in a very fine Brussels lace head-dress, a holland shift with a tucker and double ruffles of the same lace, and a pair of new kid gloves, and was then wrapped in a winding-sheet of fine linen.' Her posthumous vanity has been immortalised by Pope in the well-known lines,

> Odious! in woollen! 'twould a saint provoke
> (Were the last words that poor Narcissa spoke) ;
> No, let a charming chintz and Brussels lace
> Wrap my cold limbs and shade my lifeless face.

The law of burying in woollen was extended to Ireland[2] in 1733, but it was seldom enforced by the Irish Government, and in England it had gradually fallen into disuse long before the statutes of Charles II. were finally repealed[3] in 1814.

The Parliament of William III. made a novel use of the parish registers to replenish the exhausted Exchequer. The idea was suggested by a petition presented by the Heralds in 1693, praying that an Act might be passed to enable them to make visitations of the different counties in England and Wales, and to record in the College of Arms the pedigrees and funerals of the nobility and gentry, as they had been in the habit of doing during the Stuart reigns, under the authority of commissions from the Sovereign. The Ministers were at that time distressed for ways and means, and refused to forego this opportunity of tapping a fresh source of supply. Accordingly, amongst other taxes 'for carrying on the war against France with vigour,' a graduated scale of duties was in 1694 imposed for five years[4] upon marriages, births, and burials. For the better collection of this tax the clergy were, in 1695,[5] required under a penalty to keep a register of all births in the parish, whether the children were baptized or not. The tax-collectors were allowed to have free access to the registers without payment of fees, and the penalty of 100*l.* was incurred by the clergyman for every case of neglect in making the proper entries. Many registers, therefore, of this date are punctually kept, and the birth is usually recorded as well as the baptism. In the case of Dissenters' children born at this period, some clergymen condescended to accept certificates of baptism from Dissenting ministers, and to enter them in the parish register

---

[1] Stanley's *Westminster Abbey*, 2nd ed. p. 322.
[2] Irish Act, 7 Geo. II. c. 13.
[3] 54 Geo. III. c. 108.
[4] 6 & 7 Wm. III. c. 6.
[5] 7 & 8 Wm. III. c. 36.

for the sake of the fee.   At Foxton, Northamptonshire, several
leaves of the register from 1697 are headed—

'Those set down in the register only born were baptized by
Nonconformist ministers.'

It was found, however, that few registers could bear the test of
official inspection ; and to relieve the alarm of the clergy an
Indemnity Act[1] was passed in the next reign, confessedly on the
ground that they had, by non-compliance with the law, exposed
themselves and their families to ruin.   How much this indemnity was needed may be inferred from an incident mentioned by
Throsby in his *History of Leicestershire :*

'At one place I was told by the clerk, when I observed that the
register must be deficient, that Mr. —— kept the register lately,
and he, to *save tax, put no name down for two years.'*

The Act of 1694 was unpopular, and was suffered to expire ;
but it is remarkable that a similar experiment was attempted
unsuccessfully a few years later by our adversary Lewis XIV.
In 1707, financial distress prevailed in France, paper money
was at a discount of 53 per cent., and every expedient was
resorted to for raising money to carry on the war against the
Grand Allies.   Amongst other new taxes, duties were imposed
on baptisms and marriages ;[2] but it was found impossible to
levy them, for the peasantry formed a secret league to baptize
and marry at home without calling in the priest, and in Périgord
they rose in open rebellion.

When these Taxation Acts expired, the registration of births
was generally discontinued, and was never renewed until the new
system was established in 1836.   An unsuccessful attempt, however, was made in 1753[3] to enact an annual registration of the
whole population, with their births deaths and marriages ; and
after considerable opposition the bill passed the Commons.   But
the measure was not popular; and the proposer, Mr. Potter, did not
stand high in the public esteem.[4]   The census was regarded as
ominous and unlucky by a superstition more generally felt than
avowed ; and the register was viewed by the nation in the
odious light of a French institution ; and therefore, when the
Lords threw out the bill on the second reading, no disappoint-
ment was exhibited, and no effort was made to revive it.   The
same session is memorable for the passing of Lord Hardwicke's
Marriage Act, which with some modifications still remains the

---

[1] 4 Q. Anne, c. 12.   [2] *Memoirs of St. Simon,* ed. St. John, vol. ii. p. 97.
[3] *Parliamentary History,* xiv. 1,318, &c.
[4] *Gent. Mag.,* 1753. Thomas Potter, M.P. for Aylesbury, and son of the
Archbishop of Canterbury, was known as one of the profligate twelve who called
themselves Franciscans, and held their orgies at Medmenham Abbey.

law of the land. Up to this time a marriage by a clergyman
in Holy Orders, without banns or licence, was valid and indis-
soluble, although the parties were subject to ecclesiastical censure, and the celebrant incurred legal penalties. The rector of
St. James's, Duke's Place, was suspended for three years *ab
officio et beneficio* on February 17, 1686, for suffering persons
to be married at his church without banns or licence; but all
penalties were practically inoperative, where the clergyman had
neither liberty money nor credit to lose by any proceedings
which the bishop could institute. This was emphatically the
case within the prisons; and the Fleet in particular became
notorious for the number of clandestine marriages which were
celebrated within its precincts. It was resorted to by persons
of all ranks and conditions, from the peer to the chimney-
sweep, who desired to be married with secrecy and despatch.
When Mr. Fox, afterwards the first Lord Holland, made a runaway match in 1744 with the Duke of Richmond's daughter,
they were married at the Fleet.

FLEET REGISTERS. '1744, May 3. The Honble. Henry Fox and
Lady Caroline Lennox married.'

The Fleet Registers abound with illustrious names, but were
so irregularly kept that they have never been received in
Courts of Justice as evidence of a marriage; and if the House
of Lords was induced to admit them in the Saye and Sele
Peerage Case, it was only because the entry was corroborated by
proof that the parties were always received in good society as
man and wife. Clandestine marriages of persons of rank were
by no means confined to the Fleet; and the Duke of Hamilton's
marriage to the beautiful Miss Gunning, which was the immediate cause of the Marriage Act, was celebrated in Keith's
chapel in Mayfair:

MAYFAIR CHAPEL, LONDON. '1752, Feb. 14. James, Duke of
Hamilton, and Eliza Gunning married.'

Horace Walpole gives a lively account of the circumstances of
this marriage :—

'The Duke carried off Miss Gunning from a ball, and notwithstanding the lateness of the hour sent for the rector of St. George's,
Hanover Square, to marry them. Dr. Trebeck, however, refused
to perform the ceremony without licence and ring. The Duke
swore he would send for the Archbishop; at last they were married
with a ring of a bed-curtain at half an hour past 12 at night at
Mayfair Chapel.'[1]

Amongst other great people whose marriages are recorded
in the register of Mayfair Chapel, are the following :—

[1] *Horace Walpole's letter*, edited by Lord Dover, vol. iii. p. 51.

'1744, Sept. 4. Francis, 2nd Duke of Buccleugh (grandson of the Duke of Monmouth) and Alice Powell.'

'1751, May 25. The Honble. Sewallis Shirley and Margaret, widow of Robert, Earl of Orford (who died April 1751).'

The Fleet and Mayfair Chapel registers were not authenticated by the Commissioners appointed in 1836 to inquire into the state custody and authenticity of non-parochial registers, and it was distinctly recorded that they are deposited with the Registrar-General for safe custody only.

The Marriage Act declared all marriages contracted after March 25, 1754, to be void, unless they were solemnised by licence or banns in some church or chapel in which banns had heretofore usually been published; and every person solemnising a marriage without banns or licence, or in any other place than such church or chapel, was to be held guilty of felony, and liable to fourteen years' transportation. The Act was so stringently construed, that marriages were no longer possible in Westminster Abbey or St. Paul's Cathedral, because it had never been the custom to publish banns there; and the Court of King's Bench felt itself compelled to decide in 1781, that the prohibition extended to churches, which had been built or consecrated since the passing of the Act. The consequence was that a marriage which had been solemnised in a new church consecrated in 1765 was held to be void; and it was evident that all the clergy who had celebrated marriages in such new churches in ignorance of the law had been guilty of felony, and were liable to transportation. There were several bishops amongst them, and the decision created such a panic, that an Act was passed in the next Session to declare valid marriages solemnised in any of these new churches, and to relieve the celebrant clergy from the penalties which they had unwittingly incurred.

Lord Hardwicke's Act was, as Blackstone[1] confesses, 'an innovation on our ancient laws and constitution;' but it proved so effectual a remedy to the scandal of clandestine marriages, that every attempt to repeal it has hitherto been successfully resisted. The Act was limited to England and Wales, and was therefore evaded by a journey across the border to Scotland, where the consent of the parties before witnesses was still sufficient to constitute a legal marriage. It was not necessary, however, to travel so far north, for the Act did not extend to the Channel Islands; and it was advertised[2] in 1760 that sailing vessels were always kept ready at Southampton, which

---

[1] *Blackstone's Commentaries*, vol. i. p. 438.
[2] *Gent. Mag.*

for a fare of five guineas would carry runaway couples over to Jersey or Guernsey, where they could still be married without banns or licence.

Quakers and Jews were exempted from the provisions of the Marriage Act, but Dissenters of all other denominations were unable after 1754 to marry in their own chapels, and were compelled to have their marriages solemnised by ministers of the Church of England.

The Stamp Act of 1783[1] for the first time imposed a duty of 3*d.* upon every entry in the parish register. This was probably the most objectionable statute in the whole series. The new tax fell lightly on the rich, and pressed heavily on the poor, placing the clergyman in the invidious light of a tax-gatherer; and as the poor were often unable or unwilling to pay the tax, the clergy had a direct inducement to retain their good-will by keeping the registers defective. The Act extended to Scotland, and excited there an outburst of popular indignation.[2] The duty on entries of burial was stigmatised as a tax upon the misfortunes of the community, and was denounced as an exercise of tyranny from which even Lewis XIV. abstained in the plenitude of his power and the extremity of his distress: and as the statute virtually bestowed a premium on negligence and omissions, whole parishes, and even counties, discontinued the practice of registration. The obnoxious statute was repealed in 1794,[3] with another Act of such flagrant injustice that it cannot be allowed to pass unnoticed. At this period the registers of the Dissenters were mere private documents, inadmissible in any courts of justice. The Dissenters were encouraged to hope that if their registers were impressed with the Government stamp they would receive a public character, and be placed on an equality with the parish registers. Upon this understanding they consented to share the tax; and accordingly, in 1785, the Stamp Act was, at their own petition, extended 'to all Protestant Dissenters.'[4] But by a gross breach of faith the privilege was withheld although the price for it was received; and for nine years the Dissenters suffered without redress, if not without complaint.

It will have been observed that, except during the brief interval of the Commonwealth, the registers have hitherto continued to be an ecclesiastical and not a parliamentary institution; for the Taxation Acts simply made use of them as a convenient machinery for collecting the duties, and only subjected them to a partial and temporary control. But in

---

[1] 23 Geo. III. c. 71.   [2] Seton's Sketch.
[3] 34 Geo. III. c. 11.   [4] 25 Geo. III. c. 75.

1812 the registers became the direct subject of legislation, and the 70th canon was superseded by an Act of Parliament, which still constitutes the law for registering baptisms and burials.

The necessity for some such legislation had been gradually forcing itself on men's minds since 1800, when the Government ventured at last to bring in a bill to ascertain the population of Great Britain. There were then still some fanatics who quoted with alarm the sin of David in numbering the Jews; but pious people were reassured by Mr. Wilberforce's seconding the bill, and by the patent fact that in every other nation, Protestant and Catholic, a census had been taken without any outbreak of Divine vengeance, and with great advantage to the State. The population abstract of 1801 was based upon returns made by the clergy, and included a list of all registers between 1700 and 1800. It was discovered that in some hundreds of parishes the registers were deficient for periods varying from thirty to eighty years; and it was evident from the Report on the Public[1] Records published in the previous year, that the deficiencies could seldom be supplied from the bishops' transcripts. No remedy, however, was attempted for some years, although the Treasurer of the Navy complained that 'in innumerable instances' the wives of seamen were, from the defective state of the registers, unable to prove their marriages, for the clergy were jealous of Parliamentary interference, and opposed all legislation. The Government in 1811 proposed to place the registers in each province under the control of a Registrar-General; but the bill was denounced as hostile to the Church, and as a job for the creation of patronage. It was therefore suffered to drop; and the Act of 1812, although it was framed to conciliate opposition, was only allowed to pass on the last day of the session with the omission of many useful clauses, after being six times amended and reprinted.

This Act, commonly known as Rose's Act,[2] curiously illustrates the careless way in which bills are amended in committee. For whilst it is intituled 'An Act for the better regulating and preserving Registers of *Births*,' &c., and the 12th section mentions 'lists of births,' the registration of births is altogether omitted from its provisions; and by a ludicrous oversight the penalty of transportation for fourteen years for making a false entry is, by a subsequent clause, to be equally divided between the informer and the poor of the parish. The Act was substantially a re-enactment of the canon, with more particular

---

[1] *See* note [4], p. 11.   [2] 52 Geo. III. c. 146.

directions for its observance. The register-books were to be kept in an iron chest, in the parish church or within the residence of the rector: copies on parchment were annually to be sent to the bishop's registrar, who was to index them alphabetically for the convenience of search; and the copies were to pass free through the post. But the Act was as silent as the canon had been about fees for making, receiving, and indexing the transcripts, whilst it contained no provision to enforce on defaulting parishes or refractory registrars the performance of their duties. Nor were vestries encouraged to incur the expense of copies, when it became notorious that the transcripts were thrown together in a heap[1] unindexed and unarranged; and that a large mass of them, which had by some error or accident become chargeable to postage, had been from time to time refused by the registrars, and committed to the flames by the officials of the Post Office.

The most important change in the law, was that all future registers were ordered to be kept in books to be provided by the king's printers, according to one uniform scheme set out in the schedules annexed to the Act. Marriages had been registered since 1754 in the form prescribed by the Marriage Act, but it had hitherto been left to the clergy to record baptisms and burials as their individual notions of propriety dictated. How much has been gained or lost by the new system of uniformity will best be estimated by bringing together a series of entries, and comparing the practice of many generations.

I begin with marriages, which have always been recorded with greater care and regularity than baptisms and burials, from the obvious importance to persons of all ranks and religions of preserving legal proof of their children's legitimacy.

In the earliest registers marriages, baptisms, and burials are all entered together in order of date, without any attempt at classification. These early registers are usually in Latin, which was then the universal language of the Church and the Law as well as of scholars. But as the clergy grew more Protestant, their knowledge of Latin declined, and we are afraid that some of the old paper books were lost, because the clergy of 1603 were unable to transcribe the entries of their more learned predecessors. Latin registers were generally discontinued before the accession of Charles I., and in one of the latest of them there is a curious note in the handwriting of the vicar, which shows the growing opinion on the subject:

---

[1] Evidence of Sir T. Phillips and of Mr. Shephard, 1833.

ALL SAINTS, DERBY.[1] '1610, May 16. I see no reason why a register for English people should be written in Latin.

'RICHARD KILBIE, *Minister.*'

However, notwithstanding this note, the register of All Saints was not kept in English until several years afterwards.

CROYDON, SURREY.[2] '1551, Oct. 23. Reverendus pater Jhoēs Epūs Wynton. duxit Mariam Haymond generosam in ista ecclesia coram multitudine parochianorum p'sente Reverendissimo patre Thoma Cantuar. Archiepo cum multis.'

This marriage cost the Bishop his see in the next reign, for Dr. John Ponet was deposed from the bishopric of Winchester on the accession of Queen Mary for being married. He died in exile on April 11, 1556, at Strasburg, where he had published in 1554, in his own justification,

'A defence for the marriage of priests: an apology fully answering by Scriptures and ancient doctors a blasphemous book gathered by Dr. Stephen Gardiner and other Papists, and of late set forth under the name of Tho. Martyn, D.C.L., asserting that the marriage of priests and professed persons is no marriage, but altogether unlawful.'[3]

EAST QUANTOCK'S HEAD, SOMERSET.[4] '1560, Aug. 7. Thomas Luttrell, Esq., and Mrs. Margaret Hadley married.'

This was probably the last instance in England of the re-marriage of two persons who had been divorced on the score of spiritual relationship within the prohibited degrees.[5] Thomas Luttrell, a cadet of the Luttrells of Dunster Castle, had been, in the lax reign of Edward V. contracted to Margaret Hadley, the infant heiress of Withycombe, notwithstanding that she was the goddaughter of his mother, Dame Margaret Luttrell, which made them in the eye of the Church spiritually related as brother and sister, and canonically incapable of marrying each other. The bride came to her full age in the reign of Queen Mary, when the laws of the Church were not to be broken with impunity; and a sentence of divorce and excommunication was pronounced against the offenders. Pope Paul IV. was appealed to for a dispensation, and was not found inexorable, for divorces on this ground were a scandal which was then engaging the attention of the Reformers of the Council of Trent.[6] By the Pope's order,

[1] *Journal Archæol. Assoc.* No. xxvii.
[2] *Collectanea Topograph. et Geneal.* vol. iv. p. 91.
[3] *Athenæ Oxon.* 1721, vol. i. p. 218.
[4] *Journal Archæological Institute*, vol. xxxvii. p. 287.
[5] *See* page 4 and note.
[6] The Council decreed, Nov. 11, 1563, that there was never to be more than one sponsor, and that the tie of spiritual relationship was not to extend beyond the parents of the child baptized or confirmed. (*Concil. Trident. Decreta*, 24 Sessio, cap. ii.)

the culprits were, in November 1558, released from the sentence of excommunication by the Cardinal of St. Angelo, the Grand Penitentiary, on condition of their celebrating a new marriage in the face of the Church. The marriage, however, did not take place until after the Catholic Bishop of Bath and Wells had been deposed from his see for refusing to take the Oath of Supremacy to Queen Elizabeth, when, in order to avoid all questions of illegality, the previous contract and proceedings at Rome were ignored, and the bride was married by her maiden name.

ALLHALLOWS, LONDON WALL. ' 1598, July 20. Mr. Randall Crew, Counsellor-at-the-law in Lincoln's Inn, and Mrs. Julian Clipsbie, gentlewoman attending on my Lady of Shrewsbury, of this parish, were married.'

Before the Civil Wars, the upper servants in great house-holds were almost invariably pérsons of gentle blood and slender fortune, and were often related to their employers. Dame Mary Cordell, the widow of Sir William Cordell, Master of the Rolls, leaves by her will, dated Feb. 2, 1584–5, —

' To *my niece* Hubbard (Hobart), *my wayting woman*, a black gown and £20 in money, and "lykewise a littel jewell of golde sett with three littel stones and three perles." '[1]

Lady Hatton alleges in her complaint to the King against her husband Sir Edward Coker, in 1634,—

' Sir Walter Aston, now Lord Aston, married my waiting-woman, a gentlewoman of a good house and well allied.' [2]

Roger Bedingfield, the grand-nephew of Sir Henry Bedingfield, Kt.,[3] mentions in his will, dated Aug. 5, 1640,—

' My aged lady and *mistress* Lady Elizabeth Bedingfield, and my *master* Sir Henry Bedingfield.'

Catharine, wife of John Willson, addressed a petition in 1634 to her cousin-german Francis, Lord Cottington, the Chancellor of the Exchequer, in which she states—

' I am the daughter of James Dyer, late of Grove Park, Warwickshire, who was brother to your Lordship's brother. After my father's death I was for a while brought up by my uncle George Dyer, and by him *put to service to a mistress*, who by a blow struck on my nose dejected my fortunes in marriage. Ever since I have been enforced to take hard pains for my living as my poor husband does for his.' [4]

---

[1] Wills of Cordell family, printed in vol. i. of Dr. Howard's edition of the *Visitation of Suffolk*, 1567.
[2] *Calendar of State Papers, Domestic Series*, 1634.
[3] Wills of Bedingfield, printed in the *Norfolk Archæologia*, vol. vii. Part I.
[4] *Calendar of State Papers, Domestic Series*, 1634.

Since the Civil Wars servants have been taken from a lower class, and a feeling has grown up that domestic service is degrading to persons of gentle blood, but the old fashion still lingered in some families of the provincial aristocracy, and Dame Mary Chester, the widow of Sir Anthony Chester, the third Baronet of Chicheley, gave by her will, dated Feb. 3, 1710—

' The diamond earrings which I usually wear, and all my wearing apparel except my point-lace, to my cousin Elizabeth Richers, my waiting-woman,'

who was the great granddaughter of no less a person than Sir John Peyton, the Lieutenant of the Tower to Queen Elizabeth, and afterwards Governor of Jersey and Guernsey.[1]

ROXWELL, ESSEX. ' 1590, Dec. 6. John Williams and Anne Weston married.'
The bridegroom was the author of ' Balaam's Ass,' in which it was prophesied that the King would die, and Whitehall would be desolate and overgrown with grass before September 7, 1621. A copy of the libel, with annotations, was found in his pocket when he was arrested, and he was hanged, drawn, and quartered over against the King's Mews at Charing Cross, on May 7, 1619.[2] His wife's brother, Sir Richard Weston, was created Earl of Portland in 1633, and died Lord High Treasurer of England, on March 13, 1634–5.

Deaf and dumb persons signified their consent by signs, which were not the same in all dioceses, as the rubric contains no directions on the subject. The modern practice is to use the manual process in performing the service when both parties are deaf mutes.[3]

ST. MARTIN'S, LEICESTER.[4] ' 1576, Feb. 15. Thomas Tilsye and Ursula Russel were maryed ; and because the sayde Thomas was and is naturally deafe, and also dumbe, so that the order of the form of marriage used usually amongst others, which can heare and speake, could not for his parte be observed. After the approbation had from Thomas, the Bishoppe of Lincolne, John Chippendale, doctor in law, and commissarye, as also of Mr. Richd. Davye, then Mayor of the town of Leicester, with others of his brethren, with

---

[1] *Genealogical Memoirs of the Chesters of Chicheley*, vol. i. p. 349.
[2] Howell's *State Trials*, vol. ii. p. 1086.
[3] Mr. W. F. Mitchell and Miss Woodman, who were both deaf and dumb, were married in this way at All Saints' Church, Lewes, Sussex, on Dec. 3, 1881. The ceremony was performed by the manual process, by the Rev. W. Stainer, late Chaplain to the Royal Association in Aid of the Deaf and Dumb, whilst the Rector, the Rev. C. F. Nolloth, repeated slowly the marriage service aloud. (The *Standard* of December 5, 1881.)
[4] Nichols' *Hist. of Leicestershire*, vol. iv. appendix, p. 589.

the rest of the parishe, the said Thomas, for the expressing of his
mind instead of words, of his own accord used these signs : first, he
embraced her with his arms, and took her by the hand, putt a ring
upon her finger, and layde his hande upon his hearte, and then upon
her hearte, and held up his hands toward heaven. And to show
his continuance to dwell with her to his lyves ende, he did it by
closing of his eyes with his handes, and digginge out of the earth
with his foote, and pullinge as though he would ring a bell, with
diverse other signes.'

St. Botolph, Aldgate, London. 1618. 'Thomas Speller, a
dumb person, by trade a smith, of Hatfield Broadoake, in the
county of Essex, and Sarah Earle, daughter to one John Earle, of
Great Paringdon in the same county, yeoman, were married by
licence, granted by Dr. Edwards, Chancellor of the diocese of
London, Nov. 7, 1618, which licence aforesaid was granted at the
request of Sir Francis Barrington, knight, and others of this
place above named, who by their letters certified Mr. Chancellor
that the parents of either of them had given their consents to the
said marriage ; and the said Thomas Speller, the dumb parties'
willingness to have the same performed, appeared, by taking this
Book of Common Prayer and his licence in one hand and his bride
in the other, and coming to Mr. John Briggs, our minister and
preacher, and made the best signs he could, to show that he was
willing to be married, which was then performed accordinglie.
And also the said Lord Chief Justice of the King's Bench, as Mr.
Briggs was informed, was made acquainted with the said marriage
before it was solemnised, and allowed to be lawful. This marriage
is set down at large because we never had the like before.'

The following extract shows how man and wife sometimes
settled their differences by mutual forgiveness, before the
Divorce Court made marriage a revocable contract:

Bermondsey. 1604. 'The forme of a solemn vowe made
betwixt a man and his wife, the man having been long absent,
through which occasion the woman beinge maried to another man,
tooke her againe as followeth :—

'*The Man's Speech*: "Elizabeth, my beloved wife, I am right
sorie that I have so longe absented my sealfe from thee, whereby
thou shouldest be occasioned to take another man to thy husband.
Therefore I do nowe vowe and promise, in the sight of God and
this companie, to take thee againe as mine owne, and will not
onelie forgive thee, but also dwell with thee, and do all other duties
unto thee as I promised at our marriage."

'*The Woman's Speech*: "Ralphe, my beloved husband, I am right
sorie that I have in thy absence taken another man to be my husband ;
but here, before God and this companie, I do renounce and forsake
him, and do promise to kepe my sealfe onelie unto thee duringe
life, and to perform all duties which I first promised unto thee in
our marriage."

'*The Prayer*: "Almightie God, we beseech Thee to pardon our offences, and give us grace ever hereafter to live together in Thy feare, and to perform the holie duties of mariage one to another, accordinge as we are taught in thy holie word, for thy deare Son's sake, Jesus. Amen."

'1 Aug. 1604. Ralphe Goodchilde of the parish of Barkinge in Thames Street, and Elizabeth his wife, were agreed to live together, and thereupon gave their hands one to another, making either of them a solemn vowe so to do, in the presence of

'WILLM. STERE, Parson, EDWARD COKER, and RICD. EIRE, Clark.'

The certificate of the civil marriage of the Protector's daughter on November 11, 1657, has been printed already (see p. 16), but a briefer form of registration was more generally used. Thus:—

BILLINGBOROUGH, CO. LINCOLN. 1653–4, Feb. 2. 'Mr. Richard Toller, of Billingborou, in the countie of Lincoln, was married at Willowbee before Master Walley, Justice of the Peace for the said countie, unto Mrs. Elizabeth Brown, of Saltfleetby, spinster, according to the Act of Parliament dated the 24 Aug., whereon I did declare them to be man and wife.

'WM. BROWNLOWE.'

HIGHGATE CHAPEL, MIDDLESEX. 1658, July 15. 'The lady Anne Peerpoint, daughter to the Honble. the Marquis of Dorchester, and John Lord Rosse, son of Rt. Honble. the Earl of Rutland.'

This marriage was dissolved in 1668, by an Act of Parliament, which enabled Lord Rosse (*rectius* de Ros) to marry again during the lifetime of Lady Anne, and provided that his children by any other wife should be his heirs. This was the first example of a parliamentary divorce in England, and was warmly opposed by the Duke of York, although the King was earnest for it. The zeal expressed on this occasion by the two brothers was attributed by public opinion[1] to the King's desire to establish a precedent, which would enable him to dissolve his own marriage, and make La Belle Stuart his queen.

In an humbler rank of life marriages were dissolved without an Act of Parliament, by bargain and sale; and late in the last century the following entry was deliberately made in the toll-book kept at the Bell Inn, in Edgbaston Street, Birmingham:[2]

'1773, Aug. 31. Samuel Whitehouse, of the parish of Willenhill, in the county of Stafford, this day sold his wife, Mary Whitehouse, in open market, to Thomas Griffiths, of Birmingham, value one shilling. To take her with all faults.

SAMUEL WHITEHOUSE, MARY WHITEHOUSE; THOMAS BUCKLEY, of Birmingham,' *voucher.*

---

[1] Burnet's *Hist. of his Own Times.*   [2] *Annual Register*, vol. xvi. p. 130.

TWICKENHAM. '1665. Christopher Mitchell and Anne Colcot, married, 4 June, by permission of Sir Richard Chaworth, it being within the octaves of Pentecost.'

Marriages were prohibited by the ancient discipline of the Church during the seasons of Advent, Lent, and Whitsuntide, and the old register of COTTENHAM, CAMBS., contains this triplet in doggrel Latin :—

> 'Conjugium Adventus prohibet, Hilarique relaxat,
> Septuagena vetat, sed paschæ octava remittit,
> Rogamen vetitat, concedit Trina potestas.'

Similar lines in English are inserted in the register of EVERTON, NOTTS :—

> 'Advent marriage doth deny,
> But Hilary gives thee liberty.
> Septuagesima says thee nay,
> Eight days from Easter says you may.
> Rogation bids thee to contain,
> But Trinity sets thee free again.'

The close time was restricted to Advent and Lent by the Council of Trent,[1] but this decree had no force in England, and the Canons of the Anglican Church still forbid marriages to be celebrated between Rogation Sunday and Trinity Sunday. Such prohibitions, however, have in practice ceased to be regarded in England, and Lent has become, during the present reign, the favourite season for royal marriages.

The marriage contract was sometimes registered in the form of a solemn covenant.

ROTHWELL, NORTHAMPTONSHIRE. 1693–4. 'Wee, Thomas Humprey, of Thorpwaterfield, in yᵉ county of Northampton, and Elizabeth Bigge, of Broughten, in yᵉ same county, doe in yᵉ presence of yᵉ Lord Jesus His angeles and people, and all besides here present, solemnly give up ourselves to one another in yᵉ Lord as man and wife in a solemn marriage covenant, promising in yᵉ aforesayd awfull presence, in yᵉ strength of that grace that is in Christ Jesus, to discharge all those relative dutyes belonging to each of us respectively. In witness whereof we have set our hands and seales this 20 of February in yᵉ fifth year of yᵉ reign of our Sovereign Lord and Lady, William and Mary of England. This Covenant was solemnised in the presence of us.

RICH. BIGG.   THO. HUMPREY (L.S.).
(15 other signatures.)   ELIZ. BIGGE (L.S.).'

CHILTERN ALL SAINTS, WILTS. 1714. 'John Bridmore and Anne Selwood were married, Oct. 17. The aforesaid Anne

---

[1] *Concil. Trident.* 24 Sessio, cap. x.

D

Selwood was married in her smock, without any clothes or head-gier on.'

This was done from the vulgar error that a man is not liable for his wife's debts if he makes it patent to all the world, by marrying her with nothing on except her shift, that she brings him no personal estate.

BARKING, ESSEX. 1762, Dec. 21. 'James Cook, of St. Paul's, Shadwell, bachelor, and Elizabeth Batts, of Barking, spinster, married.'

The bride of Captain Cook, the discoverer of the Sandwich Isles, had the good sense to sign the register of her marriage, 'Elizabeth Cook, late Batts.' It was never contemplated by the authors of the Marriage Act of 1753, which prescribed the form of certificate now in use, that the bride would, after the perform-ance of the ceremony, describe herself by her maiden name, as is now commonly done.

ST. JAMES, BURY ST. EDMUNDS. 1832, Nov. 5. 'Christopher Newsam married Charity Morrell. "Charity Morrell being entirely without arms, the ring was placed upon the fourth toe of the left foot, and she wrote her name in this register with her right foot." '

I now pass to baptisms.

The baptismal registers are notoriously the most defective and imperfect of the whole series. This is partially accounted for by the large number of Protestants, who maintained that the baptism of infants was unlawful or unnecessary. Another reason was the scruple entertained by many Puritan ministers, that they were bound to satisfy themselves of the worthiness of the parents before they administered baptism to the child. The High Church clergy ridiculed such scruples; but in their zeal to put down the custom of baptizing children privately, they often refused to enter the baptisms in the register until the children were brought to church; and as this was never done in many cases, the register often remained imperfect.

The common form of baptismal entry in English had various degrees of brevity.

HAMPSTEAD, MIDDLESEX. '1609. Abigail Wade bapt. 13 Dec. (The daughter of Sir Wm Wade, Kt., Lieutenant of the Tower.)'

ALL HALLOWS, BREAD ST. '1608. John Sonne of John Mylton, Scrivener, bapt. 20 Dec.' (The Poet.)

ST. NICOLAS, NEWCASTLE. '1663. Dorothy, dau. of Thomas Fletcher, Cordwayner, bapt. 21 Dec. Sureties, Thomas Fletcher, Dorothy Errington, Mary Smith.'

HIGHGATE, MIDDLESEX. '1684. Ralph, son of Sir Francis Pemberton, Kt., and Dame Anne his wife, bapt. Aug. 27.'

WIMBLEDON. '1616, July 13, being Satterday, about half an hour before 10 of the clocke in the forenoon, was born the Lady

Georgi-Anna,[1] dau. to the Rt. Hon. Thos. Earl of Exeter and the Hon. Lady Frances Countess of Exeter; and the same Ladie Georgi-Anna was baptized 30 July, 1616, being Tuesday: Queen Anne and the Earl of Worcester Lord Privie Seal being witnesses: and the L[d] Bp. of London administered the baptism.'

This last entry accounts for the two ways of pronouncing the name of Georgiana, a standing subject of dispute. Modern orthography confounds by an uniform spelling two different names of distinct origin; the one a compound of George and Anne as in the above entry, and the other the Latin feminine of George.

Sometimes the time of birth was recorded with great precision, to assist the astrologer in casting the nativity of the child. As for example—

St. Edmund's, Dudley. '1539. Samuell, son of Sir Williame Smithe Clarke, Vicare of Duddly, was born on Friday morninge at 4 of the clocke, beinge the xxviij day of February, the signe of that day was the middle of Aquarius ♒ : the signe of the monthe ♓ ; the plenet of that day ♀ : plenet of the same ower ☿ and the morrow day, whose name hath continued in Duddly from the conqueste.'

Sometimes the quality of the parents is mentioned. Thus:

Staplehurst, Kent. '1549, June 9. This day being Whitsonday (wherein the Booke of the Common Prayer and Administration of the Sacraments and other rite and ceremonie of the Churche, after the use of the Churche of Englande begon to be executed), ther was first baptized Marie, the daughter of Richard Beseley, Parson of this Paryshe Churche, borne the last Thursday, hora fere quinta ante meridiem of his lawfull wif Jane, who were maryed the year before, and in the first day that the holly Comvnion in the English tonge (after thorder that now is was here mynystered), ther bothe with others most humblye and devoutlie comvnicating the same. The Parson christined his owne childe.'

Loughborough, co. Leic. '1581. Margaret, dau. of William Bannister, going after the manner of roguish Egyptians, was baptized the 2nd of Aprill.'

St. Giles, Cripplegate. '1582. Adam, sonne of Nicolas Wilson, *Minstrell*, bapt. 18 Nov.'

The London Minstrels were incorporated by a charter of Edward IV., and so many of them were resident in this parish at the end of the sixteenth century, that several are mentioned in every page [2] of the register.

---

[1] Bartlett's *History of Wimbledon.* This lady is misnamed Sophia Anna in *Collins' Peerage.* She was the earl's only child by his second wife, and died at the age of five.

[2] Malcolm, *Londinium Redivivum,* vol. iii. p. 295.

St. Mildred's, Poultry, London. '1610, Jan. 1. Dederj Taquoah, about y⁰ age of 20 yeares, the sonne of Caddi-biah, king of the river of Cetras or Cestus, in the cuntrey of Guinny, who was sent out of his cuntrey by his father, in an english shipp called the "Abigail," of London, belonging to Mr. John Davies, of this parishe, to be baptised. At the request of the said Mr. Davies, and at the desire of the said Dedery, and by allowance of authority, was by y⁰ Parson of this churche the first of Januarie baptised and named John.'

Tamworth, Warwickshire. 1706, June 27. 'Mary, my daughter, was publickly carried to the meeting-place of Tamworth, being the day of thanksgiving for the memorable victory obtained by His Grace the Duke of Marlborough over the Frenche at Ramile, and there baptized before the whole congregation by me, Hen. Roughley.'

St. Oswald's, Durham. '1640, 14 Feb. Ann, dau. of Thomas Forcer, Virginall Master, bapt.'

Infants baptized by the midwife are often called in the registers of the sixteenth century *creature*, or *creatura Christi*, or sometimes *children of God.* Thus:

Staplehurst, Kent. '1547. Ther was baptized by the mid-wyffe, and so buryed, the childe of Thoms. Goldham, called *Creature.*'

St. Peter's-in-the-East, Oxford. '1561, June 30, the *chylde of God* filius Ric. Stacy.'

'1563, July 17. Baptizata fuit in ædibus Mri. Humfrey filia eius, quæ nominata fuit *Creatura Christi.*'

'1563, July 17. *Creatura Christi*, filia Laurentii Humfredi, sepulta fuit eodem die.'

Such children, however, sometimes lived to be married.

Staplehurst, Kent. '1579, July 19. Marryed John Haffynden and *Creature* Cheseman yong folke.'

The midwife was bound to baptize the child at once if there was any danger of its dying before a priest could be fetched. The Roman Rubric directs the midwife not to wait for the birth in cases of imminent peril, as it was sufficient for the sacrament if the appearance of the head or any limb[1] gave proof of the child's separate life. If, contrary to expectation, the child eventually lived, the sacrament could not be repeated. The midwife was solemnly sworn[2] to the due performance of her office before she could obtain a licence, and curates were enjoined

---

[1] The doctrine that a child was sufficiently baptized by the baptism of a single limb was directly opposed to what Holinshed calls 'the damnable superstition of the natives in some corners of Ireland, where they made a practice of leaving the right arm of their infant unchristened, to the intent it might give a more ungratious and deadlie blow.'—*Holinshed's Chronicles.*

[2] For the oath of a midwife *see* Strype's *Annals*, vol. i. p. 537.

'to instruct midwives openly in the Church in the very words and form of baptism, to the intent that they may use them perfectly and none other.'

The grant of the licence was often entered in the register.

St. Finn Barr's Cathedral, Cork. '9° Nov., 1685. Joana Toogood, uxor Jooloffe Twogood de Civit. Corck, *licentiata* fuit *obstetrix* infra Civit. et Dioces. Corcag.'

The midwife sometimes made mistakes in the sex of the child. Thus:

Hanwell, Middlesex. '1731, Oct. 24. Thomas, (daughter) son of Thomas Messenger and Elizabeth his wife, was born and baptized; by the midwife at the font called a boy, and named Thomas by the godfather, but proved a girl.'

Baptized infants who died within the month after their birth were formerly shrouded in the white cloth (chrisom) put on the head at baptism, and were therefore called *Chrisoms*. The use of the chrisom is thus mentioned in the rubric of the first Prayer-book of Edward VI., 1549:

'Then the godfathers and godmothers shall take and lay their hands upon the child, and the minister shall put upon him his white vesture, commonly called the chrisom, and say, "Take this white vesture for a token of the innocency which by God's grace in this holy sacrament of baptism is given unto thee; and for a sign whereby thou art admonished, as long as thou livest, to give thyself to innocency of living, that, after this transitory life, thou mayest be partaker of the life everlasting. Amen.'

Calvin,[1] in his letter to Protector Somerset (Oct. 22, 1548), contends that the ceremony of the chrisom

'does not admit of defence, for the chrisom was the invention of a frivolous fancy of persons who were not content with the institution of Jesus Christ.'

The chrisom was accordingly expunged from the Prayer-book of 1552; but the memory of it long lingered in the hearts of the people, and down to the eighteenth century babes dying in their innocence were called Chrisoms[2] in the bills of mortality and in registers.

Westminster Abbey. '1687. The Princess Ann's child, a *chrissome*, bur. 22 Oct.'

Illegitimate children are designated in various ways. Thus:

Burwash, Sussex. '1566. Johannes, filius Thomasinæ Collins, *incerti vero patris*, bapt. 15 Dec.'

Croydon. '1567. Alice, *filia vulgi*, bapt. Aug. 14.'

'1582. William, *filius terræ*, christened May 4.'

---

[1] Gorham's *Gleanings*, 1857, p. 67.
[2] Blount's *Glossographia*, 8vo. 1670, p. 123.

HERNE, KENT. '1583. Agnes filia Bartholomæi, *fornicatoris*, bapt. 26 Jan.'

STEPNEY. '1589. Jonas, a *bastard son* of that ancient harlot, Elizabeth Duckett, of Poplar.'

BARKING, ESSEX. '1590. Fortuito, *a bastard* from Loxford, bapt. 31 Dec.'

TWICKENHAM. '1590. A *scapebegotten* child.'

SEDGEFIELD, CO. DURHAM. '1598. Forsaken, *filius meretricis* Agnetis Walton, bapt. 27 Jan.'

ISLEWORTH. '1603. Anne Twine fil. *uniuscujusque.*'

ULCOMB, KENT. '1608. Jeremias *filius scorti* de Hedcorne.'

WALDRON, SUSSEX. '1609. Flie-fornication, the *bace son* of Catren Andrews, bapt. 17 Dec.'

WEST THORNEY, SUSSEX. '1615. Spinola, the sonne of Dorothy Dumpar, *base borne*, was baptized 10 March, his god-*filius* fathers were Godfrey Blaxton, Parsone of. Thorney, *terræ* and Thomas Roman, and Widdowe Toogood, god-mother; Gods blessing be uppon him. Amen.'

MINSTER, KENT. '1620. Johanna filia Tamsin Smith *adulterina.*'

STEPNEY. '1633. Oct. 23. Alexander, son of Katherine, wife of Alexander Tuckey, of Poplar, begotten she affirmed in the field on this side the mud wall near the Gunne, about 9 of the clock at night; the father she knew not, but the said Alexander, by them that brought the child to be baptized, requested that it might be recorded in his name.'

PETERSHAM, SURREY. '1633. Nicolas, the sonne of Rebecca Cock, *filius populi*, bapt. 28 Jan.'

STOCK HARWARD, ESSEX. '1634. March 15. John, y[e] sonne of John Fisher (as was sayed), and of Margaret, a stranger brought to bed at y[e] Cocke, some four days before was baptized y[e] same time, being y[e] 15th of March pdct., on which day in y[e] night y[e] said Margaret, as they called her, and her sayed sonne were together with one, whom they called her sister, secretly conveyed away—y[e] host and hostesse not knowing hereof—*Meretricium certe hoc fuit facinus.*'

FORCETT, YORKSHIRE. '1662. Anne, *supposed* daughter of Sir Jeremiah Smithson, *fathered* of y[e] said Sir Jeremiah *in the church.*'

ALL SAINTS, NEWCASTLE. '1683. Cradock Bowe, *lovebegot.*'

LAMBETH. '1685. George Speedwell, a *merrybegot.*'

'1688. Anne, a *byeblow* in Lambeth Marsh.'

RAMSDEN BELLHOUSE, ESSEX. '1717, Jan. 13. Diana, daur. of John Billy and Diana Waker, *proles spuria.*'

ELTHAM, KENT. '1778. John Whore, a *base born* infant.'

Foundlings are of frequent occurrence. They were sometimes named by the caprice of the vestry, and we have all heard of Sir Richard Monday,[1] who 'died at Monday Place.' The following are examples of a similar nomenclature:—

---

[1] Crabbe's poem, *The Parish Register.*

St. Nicolas, Durham. ' 1548. Thos. *Nameless*, sonne of Wingblind, bapt. Nov. 22.'

' 1565. Cuthbert *Godsend* christened 17 Feb.'

St. Dunstan West, London. ' 1594. *Relictus* Dunstan, a child found, bapt. 3 Aug.'

' 1618. Mary *Porch*, a foundling, bapt. 18 Jan.'

' 1629. *Subpœna*, a child found, bur. 16 Jan.'

' 1631. Eliz. *Middlesex*, found in Chancery Lane.'

St. Helen's, Bishopsgate, London. 1612. ' Job *rakt out of the Asshes*, being borne the last of August in the lane going to Sr. John Spencer's back gate, and there laide in a heape of seacole asshes, was baptized the ffirst daye of September following, and dyed the next day after.'

St. Gregory by St. Paul's, London. 1629. 'Moyses and Aaron, two children found in the street, 26 December.'

But foundlings more often received their surnames from the parishes in which they were found.

Penn, Staffordshire. ' 1750, March 25. Mary Penn, foundling, bapt. This child was found tied up in a cloth, and hung to the ring upon the south door of Penn Church, about 8 o'clock p.m. by William Baker, as he was coming out of the church after the ringing of the curfew bell.'

Thus, in St. Lawrence's, Old Jewry, the surname of Lawrence is invariably given to them, and in St. Clement Danes[1] they are all named Clement. The same custom prevailed in Lincoln's Inn and the Temple, and it appears from the Temple register, that between 1728 and 1755 no less than 104 foundlings were baptized there, and were all of them surnamed Temple or Templar. It would be curious to ascertain how many of their descendants in this genealogical age confidently trace their origin from Leofric and Godiva, the mythical ancestors of all the Temples.[2]

It must not, however, be supposed that the true number of the parish foundlings can be estimated from the register, for entries of baptism and burial were often omitted when no fees were paid. The justices of Middlesex reported[1] in 1686, that the parish of St. Clement Danes was charged in 1679 with 16 foundlings, who were all named Clements, and that within the next six years 50 children had been found in the streets, who had all been baptized Clement; but only

---

[1] Diprose's *Hist. of St. Clement Danes*, p. 194.

[2] The Temples of Stowe were, before the suppression of monasteries, yeomen and tenants of the Abbot of Oseney. Peter Temple acquired abbey lands and had arms granted to him in 1567. The legend of their descent from the Saxon Earls of Mercia is annually repeated in that gorgeous repertory of genealogical mythology, Burke's *Peerage and Baronetage*.

a small percentage of these foundlings is noticed in the parish register.

The following entries illustrate the Anglican doctrine and practice respecting baptism :

STOCK HARWARD, ESSEX. '1635, May 3. Clemens, yᵉ daughter of John Harris, of West Hanningfield, and of Clemens his wife (uppon expresse leave given by their owne minister or curate in regard of his absence and other occasions), was baptized May yᵉ 3rd, 1635.'

HILLINGDON. '1671. Elizabeth, the dau. of Wm. Pratt, bapt. Feb. 25. The first that in 11 years was baptized with water in the font, the custom being in this place to baptize out of a bason in the Presbyterian manner, only set in the Font, which I could never get reformed, till I had gotten a new clarke John Brown, who presently did what I appointed.'

ST. ALKMUND'S, DERBY. '1712. Baptized Elizabeth and Honeylove, the daus. of John King, Nov. 5. Note.—Elizabeth was about 3 years old. The reason why she was baptized at the same time in the Church with Honeylove the infant was this, I had sometyme before preached concerning baptism, and proved that the Dissenting teachers have no authority to baptize, and consequently that children that had been sprinkled by them ought to be baptized by an Episcopal minister. The father was so fully convinced by what was said, that he came to me and desired me to baptize the said child.'

LANCHESTER. '1714. Francis Swinburne, popishly baptized 27 Jan., and no precedente.'

ST. MARY-LE-BOW, DURHAM. '1732. James Graham, a felon, bapt. 30 Aug. He was hanged yᵗ same morning, *just after his baptism.*'

Whatever number of names may be given to a child in baptism, they only make one Christian name, but it is evident from the registers that the Italian[1] custom of giving more than one name found little favour with our forefathers. I have found only one solitary instance of an Englishman bearing two names

---

[1] The Italian origin of this custom has not hitherto been noticed, but I can find no examples out of Italy before the sixteenth century. *Charles Robert*, King of Hungary, was born at Naples 1292. *John Francis* Gonzaga, Marquis of Mantua, was born 1394. *John Galeazzo* Visconti, Duke of Milan, 1395, was father of Dukes *John Maria* and *Philip Maria*. *John Francis* Pico, Count of Mirandola, died 1467. *Æneas Silvius* Piccolomini, Pope Pius II., was born at Sienna 1405. *John Baptist* Cibo, Pope Innocent VIII., was born at Genoa 1432. *Peter Guy*, Count of Guastalla, 1449, was father of Counts *Guy Galeotto* and *Francis Maria*. *Charles John Amadeus*, Duke of Savoy, was born 1488. *John Peter* Caraffa, Pope Paul IV., was born 1476. Catharine de Médicis brought this fashion into France, and her second son (who reigned as Henri III.) was baptized in 1551 *Edward Alexander*. Mary Stuart christened her only son *Charles James* after the new French fashion. Since the reign of Henri IV., no member of the royal family of France has ever been baptized by a single name, and society has almost

before the middle of the sixteenth century. *Henry-Algernon,* fifth Earl of Northumberland, whose household book is well known to antiquaries, was born Jan. 13, 1477–8,. and his double name appears on his garter[1] plate in St. George's Chapel. But it must be doubted whether the earl was christened Algernon, for at that time baptismal names were taken without exception from the saints of the Church; and it is more probable that he adopted in the pride of race the Norman sobriquet or surname of his ancestor William de Percy, who was distinguished in the court of William Rufus as William Alsgernons, or William 'with the moustache.'[2] With this doubtful exception, the first example of a double name which I have met with is in Fuller,[3] the Church historian, who says that Queen Mary gave to her godsons 'her own name in addition to their Christian names,' so that they were called *Anthony-Maria, Edward-Maria,* &c. But in the reigns of Elizabeth and James I. the use of two names was so rare in England, that not a single instance occurs amongst the 2,222 students admitted to the Inner Temple[4] between 1571 and 1625; and Camden the antiquary[5] expressly states,—

'I only remember now his Majesty, who was named *Charles James,* and the Prince his sonne *Henry Frederic*; and among private men, *Thos. Maria* Wingfield and Sir *Thomas Posthumus* Hobby.'

In the next generation a few noble ladies were named Henrietta Maria out of compliment to the queen, but a double name was regarded as a foreign fashion, and was almost confined to the royal family. The only instance which I have noticed

universally followed the example set by the court. But the Huguenots for a long time regarded it as a Popish invention, which they had scruples in accepting; and it was gravely debated by the French Protestants, in their synod in 1596, whether a child might lawfully receive two names in baptism. (Quick's *Synodicon in Gallia,* vol. i. p. 178.)

[1] Collins' *Peerage,* 1779, vol. ii. 382. The sixth earl, who died in 1537, is also called *Henry-Algernon* by Collins; but this requires proof, for he is named simply Henry in Beltz's *List of Knights of the Garter,* and in the inscription on his tomb at Hackney.

[2] This sobriquet and its Latin synonym was borne by others besides Wm. de Perci. Ranulf *Gernon,* Earl of Chester, died 1128, Eustace *Gernon,* Count of Boulogne, died 1093, and Baldwin Sieur d'Alost *Gernobadatus* died 1127. Ducange derives Gernon from Grani, which in low Latin signified the moustache, because it was twisted into points like barleycorns. The moustache (grani) is mentioned by Bp. Isidore (died 636) as the national characteristic of the Goths.

[3] Fuller's *Church History,* ed. Brewer, vol. iv. p. 249.

[4] Members of the Inner Temple, 1571–1625. 1868.

[5] *Camden's Remains,* p. 44. Another famous exception may be noted. The first Earl of Shaftesbury, born July 22, 1621, says in his autobiography, 'I was christened by the name of *Anthony Ashley.*'

in the registers[1] of Westminster Abbey before 1705 is *Frances Theresa* Duchess of Richmond (la belle Stuart), who died in 1702. The official list of Catholics 'and others who refused to take the oaths to King George' in 1715, gives the names of more than 3,100 of the English nobility and gentry, but only fifteen[2] out of the whole number have two names; and only five such instances will be found amongst the 4,990 freeholders who voted at the Lincolnshire election of 1723.[3] It appears, therefore, that in the reign of George I. not one grown-up person in two hundred amongst the aristocracy, and only one in a thousand of the general population, had more than one name.

So soon as two names had ceased to be a distinction, vanity suggested the use of three. The court again set the example, and in 1738, George III. was baptized by the names of George William Frederic. But for many years this fashion was regarded as too absurd for Englishmen to follow; and Goldsmith, in 1761, represents it as a proof of the simplicity of the Vicar of Wakefield, that he could suppose a lady of quality would be called Caroline Wilhelmina Amelia Skeggs. The same feeling is expressed in a letter, dated Dec. 12, 1764, from Gilly Williams to Geo. Selwyn.[4] He writes:

'Lord Downe's child is to be christened this evening. The sponsors I know not, but his three names made me laugh not a little—John Christopher Burton. I wish to God when he arrives at the years of puberty he may marry Mary Josephina Antonietta Bentley.'

But social changes were of quick growth in the age which saw the French Revolution, and Selwyn was still living when the following baptism was recorded:

BURBAGE, WILTS. '1781. Charles Caractacus Ostorius Maximilian Gustavus Adolphus, son of Charles Stone, tailor, bapt. 29 April.'

This string of illustrious names will have its admirers, but it cannot be said to fulfil the conditions of Mr. Weller's famous definition of 'a wery good name and an easy one to spell.' Names equally numerous and extravagant might be quoted from

---

[1] They are printed to this date in *Coll. Top. & Gen.* vols. vii. and viii.

[2] Cosins' *List of Nonjurors, &c.* in 1715. Five names out of the fifteen are more properly examples of a double surname than of two baptismal names, such as John Beaumont-Tasburgh, Christopher Cresacre-More, &c.

[3] Lincolnshire Poll Book, 1723, quoted in *Notes and Queries*, 2nd s. vol. iv. p. 376.

[4] *Memoirs of Geo. Selwyn*, by Jesse. The 'child' referred to was born Nov. 15, 1764, succeeded as fifth Viscount Downe, and died in 1832 s.p.

the books of the present Registrar-General, but it would be invidious to dwell on the follies of the uneducated in days when royal princes [1] condescend to think their dignity exalted by the possession of *fifteen* Christian names.

The very confusing custom of calling several children of the same family by the same Christian name was common enough in the Middle Ages. Sir John Hawkwood, the famous Condottiere general of the fourteenth century, had an elder brother named John; and his granddaughter, Lady Alice Tyrell, of Herons, died in 1422, leaving four sons, of whom two were named William, and the other two John.[2] This custom has long been discontinued, but it still survived in the sixteenth century. Protector Somerset had no less than three sons named Edward, who were all living at the same time; viz. Sir Edward Seymour, his eldest son (born 1529, died 1593); Edward Earl of Hertford (born 1539, died 1621); and Sir Edward the king's godson (born 1548, died 1574). John Dudley, the great Duke of Northumberland, had two sons named Henry, of whom one was slain at the siege of Boulogne in 1544, and the other at the battle of St. Quintins in 1557. John White, Bishop of Winchester, 1556–60, was brother to Sir John White, Kt., Lord Mayor, 1563. John Leland, the antiquary, had a brother John; and it appears from the will of Sir Anthony Hungerford,[3] Kt., of Down Amney, Wilts, 1558, that his eldest and youngest sons were both called John, whilst his fourth and fifth sons were both named Edward. Nor was this practice confined to the higher classes, for such entries as the following are of frequent occurrence:

BEBY, CO. LEIC. '1559, Aug. 29. John and John Sicke, the children of Christopher and Anne Sicke, were baptized.

'Item, 31 Aug., the same John and John were buried.'

Some faint trace of this custom still remains in those families which repeat a favourite name on the baptism of every son, in order that it may be borne by the head of the family in case of collateral succession. Thus, all the male descendants of Henry fifth Duke of Beaufort have Henry amongst their names; and the last two generations of the Ashleys have all been christened Anthony, as if it were an honour to the Earls of Shaftesbury to be identified with the founder of their family, the patron and accomplice of Titus Oates. In the noble family of Althann, which emigrated from Swabia into Austria in the

---

[1] It appears from the *Almanach de Gotha* that the royal families of Portugal, Brazil, and Spain have more than a dozen names each. The German princes are often contented with half a dozen.

[2] *Genealogical Memoirs of the Chesters of Chichely*, vol. i. p. 302.

[3] *Coll. Top. & Gen.* vol. vii.

sixteenth century, all the males have been christened Michael, and all the ladies Maria, for the last 300 years.[1] But the most remarkable example of this kind in history was seen in France. Gui·de Laval IV., the Crusader, obtained from Pope[2] Paschal II. (1099–1118) the singular privilege that the Sieurs de Laval should for ever be called Gui, and as a condition of inheritance should all bear that name to the exclusion of any other they might have received at baptism. The lordship of Laval descended through female heirs to some of the most illustrious[3] houses in France, but the custom was religiously observed for more than 700 years, and in 1818 Gui XXVI., Duc de la Tremoille and Sieur de Laval, still preserved by an uninterrupted succession the historic name of his ancestor.

The name given at baptism was indelible, but the Catholic Church has always reserved to itself the power of changing the baptismal name at confirmation, and amongst other instances Charles IX. of France was baptized Maximilian.[4] But after the change of religion it was a disputed point whether the laws of England would recognise the new name given at confirmation. Sergeant Thomas Gawdy, who lived in the reign of Queen Elizabeth, had two sons, who were both baptized Thomas; they were both bred to the bar, and rose to be judges; and to avoid the inconvenience of being confused with his brother, the younger Thomas changed his name to Francis when he was confirmed. He died in 1606 Chief Justice of Common Pleas, but in that scrupulous age he did not venture to use the name of Francis in his purchases and grants until the advice of all the judges had been taken that it could be safely done.[5] All scruples of this kind, however, had disappeared in the eighteenth century, for Sir Onesiphorus Paul, Bart., changed his name to George by the king's sign-manual in 1780, when he was High Sheriff of Gloucestershire.

It has often been said, that the use of surnames as Christian names is a modern fashion; but the registers show that it has been a frequent practice in England since the reign of Henry VIII. Lord *Guildford* Dudley, the husband of the ill-fated

---

[1] John Michael, Count Althann, who died in 1722, was the husband of the celebrated beauty, who was the mistress of the Emperor Charles VI., and played so conspicuous a part in the political and diplomatic intrigues of her time. (Vehse's *Memoirs of the Court of Austria*, translated by F. Demmler, vol. ii. p. 114, 8vo. London, 1856.)

[2] Ménage, *Hist. de la Maison de Sablé*, fol. 1683, p. 159.

[3] *L'Art de vérifier les Dates*, 8vo. 1818, vol. xiii. 110–41.

[4] Charles IX. was not the only one of his family who changed his name at confirmation, for his brothers Edward-Alexander and Hercules changed their respective names in 1565 to Henry and Francis. (*L'Art*, vol. vii. p. 179.)

[5] Coke upon Littleton, 3 a.

Jane Grey, will at once occur to the reader; and there are many
other examples in the sixteenth century. *Poynings* Heron, of
Addiscombe, was born in 1548; *Besil* Fettiplace was Sheriff
of Berks in 1583; Sir *Hewet* Osborn was born in 1567; Sir
Multon Lambarde was born Oct. 15, 1584, and his brothers
Gore and *Fane* Lambarde were born in 1587. *Peyton* Monins
was, in 1589, the wife of Geo. Toke, Esq. *Fitz-Walter*,
son of John Hungerford, was baptized at Hungerford, Aug.
26, 1591; and Sir *Olliph* Leigh was buried at Addington,
March 15, 1611-12. But this custom was confined to Protestants, and was never heard of before the change of religion.
Up to that time baptismal names had been invariably taken
from the Calendar of the Saints; and zealous Catholics observed
this rule so strictly, that Arthur Faunt[1] the Jesuit changed in
1575 his name from Arthur to Laurence, ' because no calendar
saint was ever named Arthur.'[2] The Puritans, on the other hand,
insisted on the exclusive use of names taken from the Bible,
and Snape, who was one of their leading ministers, positively
refused in 1589 to baptize a child by the profane name of
Richard.[3] Even Scripture names, which had been included in
the Popish calendar, were distasteful to extreme Protestants,
who showed a marked preference for Jewish names, and especially for those of notorious sinners, which had been always
shunned by Catholics as names of evil omen. The Puritans
gloried in names of this kind, as bearing testimony to the tri-
umph of grace over original sin in the Christian[4] dispensation.
This notion made Ananias and Sapphira favourite names with
the Presbyterians; and Archbishop Leighton, who was the son
of a minister of this persuasion, had a sister Sapphira.

The fashion of christening by surnames was recommended to
Protestants by the double attraction of violating an old Catholic
precept, and of gratifying the love of singularity. But this
departure from the practice of antiquity offended the prejudices
of many staunch Protestants of the old school, and was charac-
teristically regarded by Sir Edward Coke with mingled feelings

---

[1] Fuller's *Church History*, ed. Brewer, v. 177.

[2] The same scruple still flourishes amongst the Ultramontane clergy. In 1858
a Catholic solicitor at Bayswater wished his son to be christened Geoffrey; but
the neighbouring priest objected, that no saint of that name could be found in the
calendar. It was suggested that Geoffrey was a family name of the Plantagenets
in the ages of faith, and was constantly used in Catholic France. But clerical
scruples are seldom dissolved by lay reasoning: the parents were converts, and
had exhausted their energies of remonstrance in the act of conversion; so by way
of compromise the child was christened Godfrey after the crusading King of
Jerusalem, whom the priest probably considered a saint.

[3] Collier's *Ecclesiastical History*, vol. vii. p. 130.

[4] Neal's *History of the Puritans*, 1822, vol. i. p. 194.

of dislike and superstition. He gravely notes it as the result of his experience, that most people who had received surnames in baptism had turned out unfortunately. But Fuller[1] (the historian), a writer of the next generation, remarks with equal gravity, that the practice was then a ' common ' one, and that ' the good success of many men so named had confuted the truth of Coke's observation.' Since the civil war this usage has been too general to require comment or illustration.

It remains to notice Burials.

The burial registers are less imperfect, and have been better kept than the baptismal, because Dissenters of every denomination were unwilling to be excluded from the parish churchyards in which their ancestors were laid. The new statutory form supplies the valuable addition of the age and residence of the deceased, but the ancient entries are often very quaint.

St. Peter's in the East, Oxford. '1568. There was buried Alyce, the wiff of (a naughtie fellow whose name is) Mathew Manne.'

Staplehurst, Kent. '1578. There was comytted to the earth the body of one Johan Longley, who died in the highway as she was carryed on horseback to have been conveyed from officer to officer, tyll she should have come to the parish of Rayershe.'

This entry shows how strictly the inhuman law of Edward VI.[2] was enforced, for removing the aged and infirm poor to the place of their birth or last residence.

St. Martin's, Ludgate. '1615, Feb. 28, was buried an *anatomy* from the College of Physicians.'

Attleburgh, Norfolk.[3] 1625, Aug. 11. ' Then was buried Mary, wife of Gilbert Greene, hoastess of the Cock, who knew how to gain more by her trade than any other, and a woman free and kind for any in sickness or woman in her travail or childbed, and for answering for anyones child, and readie to give to anyones marriage.'

Ripe, Sussex. '1634. I buried Alice Whitesides Feb. 22 who being but one weeke in the parish of Ripe, died as a stranger. for whose mortuary, I, John Goffe, had a gowne of Elizabeth her Daughter, price 10ˢ.'

The exaction of *mortuaries* or *corse presents* ' from travelling and wayfaring men in the places where they fortuned to die,' was expressly forbidden by statute (21 Hen. viii. c. 6).

Stock Harward, Essex. 1642. ' That vertuous : religious : humble : and trulie charitable Gentlewoman, Mrs. Juliet Coo, the wife of William Coo Esquire, departed this mortall life in the Cittie

---

[1] Fuller's *Worthies,* ed. Nuttall, vol. i. p. 159.
[2] 3 & 4 Edward VI. c. 16.
[3] Blomefield's *Hist. of Norfolk,* 8vo. vol. ii. p. 536.

of London on Wednesday May 18. And was from thence conveyed in a coach to this Towne where she dwelt : And was there solemnly interred (as beseemed her ranke), in the chancell belonging to this Parrish Church on Friday May 20, Where her worth and eminent vertues (to her eternall Memory) were both elegantlie and trulie related in a learned-funerall-sermon, By that Reverend Man of God Mr. William Pindar, Rector there.'

' This breefe commemoration was entered by THOMAS CHITHAM, *Church Clarke.*'

WADHURST, SUSSEX. ' 1674. Damaris, the wife of Robert Gower, was buried Nov. 1 (sine exequiis sepulta, non ob malum morale, sed ob infectionem morbillorum) a good Christian.'

KYLOE, NORTHUMBERLAND. ' 1696. Bur. Dec. 7. Henry, y° son of Henry Watson of Fenwick, who lived to the age of 36 yeare, and was so great a fooll, that he never could put on his own close, nor never went a quarter of a mile off y° house, in all this space.'

RAMSDEN BELLHOUSE, ESSEX. '1708. Maria Feast sepulta est 4 Cal. April. Epulum (si Deus voluerit) vermibus nimis delicatum. Erat enim satis venusta.' ·

ST. GEORGE'S, BLOOMSBURY. ' 1715. Robert Nelson, Esq., buried 24 Jan.'

The learned and pious author of ' Fasts and Festivals ' was the first person who was buried in the new cemetery of St. George's, which was on the Uxbridge Road, just beyond Tyburn. It faces Hyde Park, in the heart of what is now one of the most fashionable quarters of London, but was then so desolate and remote from human habitation that public opinion was strongly prejudiced against it as a burial-place, and it was hoped that the interment of so eminent a Christian would make it less unpopular.[1]

CROYDON. ' 1788. Mary Woodfield al* *Queen of Hell*, from the college, bur. 18 Feb.'

ST. BARTHOLOMEW, BROAD STREET, LONDON. ' 1581. Mr. Francis Bowyer, Alderman, buried in St. Michael's Church ; but the solemnities of his funeral were ministered in this, 7 Aug.'

It was not unusual, when persons of consequence died, to have the funeral service performed with a *corpus fictum*, or effigy of the deceased, in all the different churches with which they were connected, and such funerals were entered in the parish register as if they were actual burials, although the body was interred elsewhere. Queen Elizabeth was buried in this way in all the London churches ; and the register of Selborne, Hants, records in 1594 the burial of Thomas Cowper, Bishop of Winchester, although he was actually interred in his own cathedral church.

[1] Nichols' *Literary Anecdotes*, vol. iv. p. 190.

Solemn burials were directed and served by the Heralds, who drew up funeral certificates, which were subscribed by the executors of the deceased, and were recorded in the College of Arms. The series of these certificates begins in 1567, and for genealogical purposes they are of equal value and authority to the Visitations, which were made by the Heralds under royal commissions; but they have been discontinued since the Revolution of 1688, and the Heralds have long ceased to attend, except at royal and public funerals, at which they still marshal the procession, and proclaim the style of the deceased.

After the change of religion masses and prayers for the souls of the dead were superseded by a funeral sermon and a burial feast, for which persons of condition usually made provision in their wills. For example, William Methoulde, citizen and mercer, of London, by his will,[1] dated April 25, 1580, gave ten shillings to the Vicar of St. Lawrence in the Old Jewry, 'for the sermon on the day of my funeral;' and directed that 'the people, poor and rich, dwelling in the alley of Milk Street in our end of the parish of St. Lawrence be feasted on the day of my funeral; some at dinner and the rest at supper,' and 40*l.* was to be expended on their entertainment. This feasting at funerals, however, was not a Protestant innovation, for something very like an Irish wake was in the Tudor reigns not unknown in England. James Cooke, of Sporle, Norfolk, says in his will[2] in 1528,—

'I will that myn executors as soon as it may come to ther knowleg that I am dede, that they make a drynkyng for my soul to the value of vi*s.* viii*d.* in the church of Sporle.'

The burial feast went out of fashion in the seventeenth century, but there was always a funeral sermon, after which wine, wafers, gloves, and rosemary were distributed. This distribution was so much a matter of course at all funerals of the better class, that Smyth thought it worth noting in his *Obituary* that Mr. Cornelius Bee, a bookseller in Little Britain, 'was buried on 4 Jan. 1671–2, at St. Bartholomews the Great,[3] without a sermon, without wine or wafers; only gloves and rosemary.'

ISELHAM, CAMBS. '1590. Mr. Robert Peyton, Esquier, died 19 Oct., and was solemnely buried 12 Nov. next following.' He is wrongly styled a knight in all the Baronetages, and

---

[1] 27 Arundell in Prerog. Court of Canterbury.
[2] Suckling's *Hist. of Suffolk*, vol. i. p. 42.
[3] Smyth's *Obituary*, p. 93. Camden Society.

married one of the daughters of Lord Chancellor Rich, who died in the next year.

'1591. Mrs. Elizabeth Peyton, widow, late wife of Mr. Robert Peyton, Esquier, died 17 Oct., and was *solemnely* buried 26 October.'

The preparations for the solemn burial necessarily took up much time, so that the funeral was often postponed for several weeks after the interment; and it will be seen from the next entry, that in the case of Sir Edward Clere, who died on June 8, 1606, and was buried at Blickling on June 21, the solemn funeral was not celebrated until the following August 14.

BLICKLING, NORFOLK. '1606. Dnus Edwardus Clere miles, quondam Dnus de Blickling, obiit Londinii 8vo die Junii, atque sepultus fuit apud Blickling 21° die mensis predicti, cujus funera summa *cum solemnitate* celebrata fuere 14° die Augusti, A.D. 1606.'

When persons of rank died in one parish and were buried in another, the burial was usually recorded in the registers of both parishes:

BLICKLING, NORFOLK. '1615. Robert Cleere, Esquire, and if he had survived his mother, Dame Agnes, should have been lord of Blickling, died at his lodging in Fleet Street in London on June 27. A gentleman in that riotous age of admirable temperance and holiness of life; one given to no kind of sports or play, mostly keeping his chamber in reading fasting and prayer, very studious from his childhood, and of a tender conscience. He died without issue, being never married, in the 34th year of his age, leaving his brother, Sir Edward Cleere,[1] Kt., for his heir. He was buried in the chancel near unto the Communion Table of the parish church of St. Bridget, commonly called St. Bride's, in Fleet Street, in London, on 28 June, 1615.'

Before the Civil Wars distinctions of rank were punctiliously observed in the accessories of funeral pomp. Banners of arms were reserved to peers of the realm and their wives; but standards four yards long were allowed to knights, and penons of arms to esquires; gentlemen of lower degree used only scocheons of arms. The rich citizens of London, however, were enabled to increase their funeral pomp by displaying penons of the arms of the City, and of the different companies to which they belonged; whilst all the great City companies kept magnificent berse cloths for the use of their members. This custom was not interrupted by the change of religion, for it was

---

[1] This Sir Edward Clere, the eldest son and heir of the Sir Edward, who died in 1606, is ignored altogether in Burke's *Extinct Baronetage*. It was the son, and not the father, who sold Blickling in 1616 to Sir Henry Hobart.

in 1572, long after the accession of Queen Elizabeth, that John Cawoode, the printer, left by will to the Stationers' Company 'a herse-cloth of cloth of gold, pouderyd with blew velvet, and bordered aboute with blacke velvet embroidered and steyned with blew, yellow, red and green.'

Some of these herse cloths are still in existence, and that of the Fishmongers' Company, which is elaborately embroidered with designs representing passages in the life of St. Peter, the patron saint of the Company, is engraved in Miss Lambert's volume on *Church Needlework.* The herse for which these cloths were made had nothing in common with the funeral carriage now called a hearse. It was a frame made of timber, and covered with black, which was erected within the church ready for the reception of the corpse. The church was hung with black, and the herse decked with streamers and scocheons of arms, blazed with a profusion of wax tapers during the obsequies.[1] Such costly funerals were almost universal in the Elizabethan age; and Thomas Smythe of Ostenhanger, the ancestor of the Lords Strangford, who amassed great wealth by farming the Customs of the Port of London under Queen Elizabeth, stands almost alone in his direction to be buried 'without any of such vain funereal pomp as the world, by customs in times of darkness, hath long used, but rather that all superfluous cost be spared, and the same bestowed upon the poor.' Considering the sumptuous monument in Ashford Church, which still preserves the memory of Customer Smyth, it is highly improbable that expense was spared in his funeral. Public opinion at that period reckoned it as an offence against decency and good feeling, if personages of rank were buried without the solemnities and funeral pomp suitable to their quality and to the offices which they had filled. Aldermen of London who had filled the office of Lord Mayor were, by ancient custom, buried with special solemnity, and usually by torchlight. But these nocturnal funerals were so often scenes of riot and disorder, that they were at last prohibited by Charles I. A curious letter on this subject has been preserved in the College of Arms. It was written by the Earl Marshal to the Lord Mayor on July 16, 1635, on the occasion of the death of Alderman Sir Richard Deane, who had served as Lord Mayor in 1628.

'My very good Lord,
Whereas I am informed that Sir Rich: Deane, Kt. Ald[n] and late Lo. Mayor of the Citty of London is lately deceased and to be

---

[1] The herse of Abbot Islyppe at Westminster, with all its lights burning, is engraved in the *Vetusta Monumenta.*

buryed as I am given to understand in a private manner no way sutable with his degree and eminent quality of chief magistrate of the citty not only contrary to the laudible custome of his predecessors but allsoe to yor owne constitutions made amongst yor selves for the solempne and ceremonious enterment of such as have borne office in the place of Lo: Mayor fforasmuch as his Mătie hath lately signefied his expresse pleasure and cõmand for the prohibitinge all nocturnall funeralls whatsoever for the suppression of which disorders as I am obliged by the place I hold to be carefull in the execution of his Măties Royall cõmand so am I likewise as formerly I have done in the like case ernestly to desyre your lo^p and the Executors of the defunct whom it may concerne to see the auncient and reuerend ceremonies at the enterm^t both of this gent: deceased & those of his qualety in the citty, to be decently celebrated & duly observed according to the accustomed solemnities and with vsuall rights to the memory of the deceassed. So not doubting of yor redinesse herein I rest

Yo^r lo^{ps} very loving freind

ARUNDELL & SURREY.

Arundell House 16 July 1635.

To my honorable freind

The lo: Mayor of the Citty of London.'

'The ancient and reverend ceremonies' customary at the interment of an Alderman, who had been chief magistrate of the City, are described in a contemporary account of the funeral of Sir William Roche, who was Lord Mayor in 1540, and died on September 12, 1549 :—

'The right worshipfull Sir William Roche knight & alderman, decessyd betwene ix. and x. of the clock before none. On whose soule Jesu have mercye. Amen.

'He was buryed the xvth daye of September 1549 at afternone, in this wyse. First ij. branchys of whyte wax were borne before the priests and clerks in surplesys syngyng. Then a standard of his crest, which was the red roobuck's hedd, with gylt hornes, havyng also ij. wynges, the one of gold, the other verde. Thereafter certayne mourners; then a pynion of his armys, and his cote armour, borne by the herald, which armys was a cheker of Warren of sylver and azure, a bull passaunt goules, with hornes of sylver, and iij roches, also sylver, being all sett in a felde of gold. Then the corps borne next after the cote armure, by certayne clerks, and iiij of the assystans of the 'Drapers, viz. Mr. Warner, Mr. Blower, Mr. Spencer, and Mr. Tull, who went in their livery and hodes about the said corps. Ther followyd the corse Mr. John Roche his sone, as chief mourner, alone; and after hym ij coples of mourners more. Then the sword-berer and my lord maire in black. Then the aldermen and sheriffs after them, and the hole lyvory of this felowshippe, in order. Then the ladys and gentylwomen, as the aldermen's wyfes and others, which, after

dirige, cam home to his house and dranke, where they had spice-
brede and comfetts, wyne, ale, and beere.

'On the morrow, the mourners went again in order to the
church, where they had a collacion made by Sir Stephen. After
which collacion the herald appointed the chief mourners, in order,
to offer up the target, sword and helmet, to the priest; and after
they offered in order, and also my lord mayor, the aldermen, the
livery, and others, which offering went to the poor. Then the
whole communion was ministered. After which done, the herald
again going before, there followed him the banner-bearers, and
offered the banners also; and then, in order, again the mourners,
my lord mayor, and others, returned to the house of the said Mr.
Roche, where they dined all, save the livery of this fellowship,
which dined in the Drapers' Hall, by reason he had given them
towards the same vjl. xiijs. iiijd. which was bestowed by John
Quarles and William Berwyck, stewards for the same, the xvj. day
of September, in eight mess of meat, as follows: First, brawn &
mustard, boiled capon, swan roast, capon & custard. The second
course, pidgeons and tarts, bread, wine, ale, and beer. And my lady
Roche, of her gentylnes, sent moreover four gallons of French wine,
and also a box of wafers and a pottell of ipocras.

'For whose soul let us pray, and all Christian souls. Amen!'

The trade of an undertaker is modern, and was unknown
in England before the Revolution of 1688. It arose out of the
desire to retrench the enormous expenses incurred in funerals,
when it was the custom for families to provide their own
cloaks, hangings, coach coverings, and other furniture for every
funeral. The author of a rare tract on *The Present State of
Trade*,[1] published in 1698, enumerates amongst

'The projects of late that have obtained reputation to the
prejudice of manufacturers, the furnishing of funerals by a small
number of men called *undertakers* . . . by which invention one
cloak and other necessaries serve several years and furnish some
hundred funerals . . . Since this method has got footing persons of
ordinary rank may for the value of £50 make as great a figure as
the nobility and gentry did formerly with the expense of more than
£500 . . . so that it is clear that 20 or 30 of these undertakers do
greatly hinder the consumption of our woollen manufacture, and
consequently destroy the livelyhoods of many thousand families.'

There is evidence, however, that the new system did little to
reduce the cost of funerals in the next century, for when Andrew
Card died, the senior bencher of Gray's Inn, he was buried at
St. Andrew's, Holborn, on March 6, 1731–2, and the following
bill for his funeral was delivered to his widow by the Company
of Upholsterers at Exeter Change, from which it will be seen

---

[1] *Some Considerations offered relating to our Present Trade*, by T. T. Merchant,
London, 1698, small 4to. (*Lansdowne Tracts.*)

what etiquette required to be spent in the reign of George II.
when a barrister of high standing was buried with the funeral
pomp suitable to his condition.

	£	s.	d.
A superfine pinked shroud	1	5	6
A large sarsnett sheet to wrap the body in . . .	2	10	0
An Elm Coffin, lined with a fine sarsnet quilt, a pink'd Ruffle, a sarsnet pillow run with green Inscar, and his Body put up with sweet powders . .	2	10	0
A leaden Coffin with a leaden plate of Inscription .	6	6	0
A large elm case, covered with rich black velvet, 4 pair of Chaced handles gilt & finished with the best nails close drove all round	15	0	0
A Depositum with his arms &c. curiously engraved on a Brass plate, and richly burnished, for the velvet case	2	10	0
A Room for his Body hung in deep mourning with velvet, the floor covered	10	0	0
The next room for Company hung in mourning with black cloth, the floor covered	3	10	0
The passage & stairs hung in mourning	2	0	0
A large neue velvet pall laid over his body . .	1	0	0
12 silk Escutcheons for do	3	0	0
A Coffin lid covered with velvet, & adorned with Plumes of fine black Ostrich Feathers on the body	1	1	0
A Bail round the body covered with Plumes of fine Ostrich feathers	2	2	0
8 Large Plate Candlesticks on stands round the body .	1	0	0
53 Plate Sconces for the Rooms, Passage & Stairs .	2	13	0
A Large Majesty Escutcheon with the crest and mantling painted on silk to put up at the head of the Corpse	3	3	0
12 Silk Escutcheons for do & the Rail . . .	3	0	0
43 lbs. of wax Lights and Tapers at 2/8 . . .	5	14	8
8 Doz. of Buckram Escutcheons for Rooms, Passage, & Stairs	12	0	0
8 Doz. of crests to intermix with the Escutcheon .	8	8	0
6 Rich Luttstring Scarves covered with Frizancer for the Gentlemen who supported the Pall . .	9	0	0
4 ditto longer for Divines	6	10	0
21 Alamode Hatbands covered with Frizancer for Pall-bearers, Divines and others invited, at 10/6 .	11	0	6
8 Pairs of Men's fine diamond looped Shamy gloves, at 6/6	2	12	0
11 Fine Cloaks for Mourners	1	2	0
23 Pair of Men's Shamy gloves for servants of the family officers of Grays Inn, the Club & Sexton of St. Andrews and others, at 3/6	4	0	6
15 best Crape hat bands for the same, at 3/6 . .	2	12	6
12 Pairs of Womans Shamy Gloves	2	2	0
A Hearse & six Horses	1	0	0

	£	s.	d.
8 Mourning Coaches & six horses at 18/6 . . .	7	8	0
23 Plumes of fine black ostrich Feathers for yᵉ Herse and Horses	3	10	0
Covering for yᵉ Herse and velvet housings for yᵉ Horses	3	15	0
24 buckram Escutcheons, 12 shields, 6 Shafferoons, 24 long Pencills, 24 Crests & 8 Banners on Buckram with the arms on both sides for Herse and Horses	13	6	0
9 Cloaks for Coachmen	0	9	0
18 Hatbands for ditto and Postillions	1	7	0
10 Pair of Black Gloves for ditto	0	18	0
4 Porters at the door in proper habitts to walk before the herse	1	4	0
4 Hatbands for ditto	0	4	0
12 Bearers with velvet caps and truncheons to attend the herse and horses	1	4	0
12 Prs of Gloves & 12 black knots for do . . .	1	4	0
15 Pages in mourning to attend the Coaches . .	1	10	0
A Man in mourning to carry the Coffin lid of feathers before the herse	0	2	6
100 white wax branch lights, & 100 men in mourning to carry them, at 5/6	27	10	0
100 pair of black Gloves, & 101 Knots for lightmen and Man that carried the lid of feathers . . .	7	11	6
14 pair of men's dyed drawn top'd Gloves bound with Ribbon for Gentlemens Servants and others . .	1	8	0
14 second best hat bands for ditto, at 3/ . . .	2	2	0
4 Pair of Woman's white Kid Gloves	0	8	0
8 Pair of men's Ashcoloured top'd gloves pointed and wetted with black for Porters at Grays Inn .	0	12	0
6 Bearers that brought the body out of the house, & put it into the herse, & afterwards bore it to the grave	0	12	0
2 Men to light the Porters at the door . . .	0	2	0
2 Silk hatbands and scarfs for the persons, that managed the funerall	2	5	0
9 yards of superfine fine black cloth for the Pulpit, reader's and Clerke's desk, 18ˢ	8	2	0
100 yards of pressed Baze for St. Andrews Ch. . .	8	6	8
12 Silk Escutcheons for the Pulpit	3	0	0
6 Dozen of Buckram Escutcheons for the Church .	9	0	0
6 Dozen of Crests to intermix with ditto, at 21/ . .	6	6	0
An Atchievement for the house with the outside frame in mourning	3	10	0
Ticketts printed from a new copper plate to invite the company & men in mourning to deliver them .	0	15	0
Men to help move the body downstairs . . .	0	6	0
6 Men to carry in the leaden Coffin & put the body in	0	6	0
4 Men to carry in the velvet case to put the leaden Coffin in, & fix it up	0	4	0

	£	s.	d.
4 servants in mourning to attend the funerall . .	0	10	0
Paid the parish dues of St. Andrews . . .	2	14	4
Paid the information for Burying in velvet . .	2	10	0
Six pair of black gloves for the parish bearers . .	0	6	0
Paid the stonecutter	2	4	0
Paid the bricklayer	0	10	6
Paid the men for emptying the vault of Water &c. .	0	7	6
Paid for Wine and bottles	1	19	6
Gave St. Andrews bearers	0	3	0
Gave the Stonecutters man & labourer for Expedition	0	2	0
Gave the bricklayers man & labourer	0	1	0

£269 7 11

May 13, 1732. Received of Mrs. Card the sum of £269. 7s. 11d., in full of this bill for the use of Mr. Calcott & Company.

£269.   Pr. THOMAS HARCOURT.'

The etiquette of the eighteenth century forbade the nearest relations to follow the body to the grave, and in the description of Alderman Sawbridge's funeral in 1795 the attendance of the brother and sons of the deceased is recorded[1] as remarkable by his biographer (Rev. P. Parsons, M.A., of Wye, Kent).

'The tenantry and domestics weepingly followed the hearse. And be it long, very long remembered, that in *honorable defiance* of modern fashions, the funeral rites of Mr. Sawbridge were *personally attended* by his dearly beloved brother and two sons; it being, in their estimation, the last proof of their respect to their highly valued relative, to shed a tear over his grave.'

The same notion formerly prevented the husband from seeing his wife buried in Scotland, and Lord Campbell tells us in his Autobiography[2] that when his mother died in 1793, he and his brother were chief mourners, 'as the customs of Scotland did not permit their father to attend the funeral.' The universal practice in Italy of deserting the dead to the care of servants as soon as the breath of life has left the body, still excites the surprise and indignation of English travellers.

Sometimes the cause and manner of death is mentioned:

ALL SAINTS, DERBY. '1556, Aug. 1. A poor blinde woman called Joan Waste of this parish, a *martyr*, burned in Windmill Pit.' She was condemned[3] by Ralph Baynes, Bishop of Coventry and Lichfield, and the death of this poor creature is the chief blot on the fame of that eminent scholar.

RICHMOND, CO. YORK. '1558. Richard Snell b'rnt, bur. 9 Sept.'

[1] *Gent. Mag.* vol. lxv. p. 218.
[2] *Lord Campbell's Life*, by Mrs. Hardcastle, 1881, vol. i. p. 19.
[3] Fuller's *Church Hist.* ed. Brewer, vol. iv. p. 191.

Fox the martyrologist says:

'Two of the Snells were taken up for their religion. One, after his toes were rotted off by lying in prison by order of Dakins the Bishop of Chester's Commissary, and so went upon crutches, at last went to mass, having a certain sum of money given him by the people; but in three or four days after, drowned himself in a river called Swail, by Richmond. The other Snell was burned.'

LOUGHBOROUGH. '1579. Roger Shepherd was slain by a lioness which was brought into the town to be seen of such as would give money to see her. He was sore wounded in sundry places, and was buried the 26 Aug.'

CROYDON, SURREY. 1585. 'Wyllyam Barker, a common drunkard & blasphemer, beinge drinkinge tyll he was drunken, was found dead on the xixth day of September, he being soe, he was layd in a grave, & not covered tyll the xxiind day of the same month for the crowener to vew, and then was covered.'

ST. OSWALD'S, DURHAM. '1590.

Duke			Seminaryes		to	were hanged and
Hyll			Papysts		hyr	quartered at Dry-
Hogge	iiij		Tretors		Mages-	burne for there
Holiday			and Rebels		tye	horrible offences the
						27 day of May.'

'Their horrible offences' consisted in the fact, that, being subjects of the Queen, born in England, and ordained Priests of the Church of Rome, they had remained in their native country, which by the Statute of 27 Elizabeth subjected them to the penalties of high treason. After their execution,

'their quarters were promiscuously thrown into a cart and hung up upon the gates of the city of Durham, and upon the bridges and castle, so that it could not be distinguished which were which: yet divers of them were stolen away by Catholics to be preserved as[1] relics.'

The Rector of the English College[2] at St. Omer writes:

'June 4, 1686. We have an arm of one of these four martyrs, which we keep as a most precious treasure, yet we know not to which of them it belongeth.'

Their death was long remembered, and local tradition affirms that Dryburne brook, which flowed near the gallows, was miraculously dried up on the day of their martyrdom.[3]

The cost of these cruel executions will be seen in the following extracts from the accounts[4] of the Corporation of Newcastle-on-Tyne, on the occasion of a priest being executed in 1592 under the same barbarous law.

[1] Challoner, *Missionary Priests*, 8vo. 1741.
[2] Foley's *Records of the English Jesuits*, vol. iii. p. 105.
[3] Sir Cuthbert Sharpe's *Chronicon*, p. 10.
[4] *Life of Mr. Barnes*, Surtees Society, p. 293.

'Paid to a Frenchman which did take forth the seminary priests bowels after he was hanged, 20*s.*; for coals which made the fire at the execution of the seminary priest, 6*d.*; and for a wright's axe which headed the seminary, 4*s.* 6*d.*; for a handaxe and a cutting-knife which did rip and quarter the seminary priest, 14*d.*; and for a horse which trailed him from off the sled to the gallows, 12*d.*; for four iron stanchels, with hooks on them for the hanging of the seminaries four quarters of four gates, 3*s.* 8*d.*; for one iron wedge, for riving wood to make the fire on the Moor, 18*d.*; and for a shovel to the fire, 2*s.*; to a mason for two days' work, setting the stanchels of the gates fast, 10*d.* a day, 20*d.*; for carrying the four quarters of the seminary priest from gate to gate and other charges, 2*s.*; for fire and coals for melting the lead to set the iron stanchels of the gate fast, 8*d.*'

St. Nicholas, Durham. '1592, 8 Aug. Simson, Arington, Fetherstone, Fenwicke, and Lancaster, were hanged for being Egyptians.'

These unfortunate wretches suffered death under the Statute of Elizabeth,[1] which made it a capital felony ' to continue for one month in any company or fellowship of vagabonds commonly called Egyptians.' This law was not repealed until 1783, when it was declared in the Repealing Act,[2] that ' it is and ought to be considered as a law of excessive severity.'

St. Leonard's, Shoreditch. '1598. Gabriell Spencer being slayne, was buryed 24 Sept.'

This was the player who was killed in Hoxton Fields by Ben Jonson.

St. Andrew's, Newcastle-on-Tyne. ' 1640. 2 sogers for denying the king's pay was by a counsel of war appoynted to be shott att, and a pare of gallos set up before Thos. Malaber's dore in the Byg-market, they kast lotes which should dy and the lotes did fall of one Mr. Anthone Viccars, and he was set gainst a wall and shott at by 6 lyght horsemen and was buryed in our church-yarde the sam day, 16 May.'

' 1640, Oct. 25. One of the *Redshankes* of the Skottes arme was bur.'

Charles I. marched into Newcastle, May 5, 1640, and stayed there 12 days. The royal garrison retreated on Aug. 29, and the next day the Scots took possession of the town.

St. Andrew's, Newcastle-on-Tyne. '1650, 21 August. Thes partes her under named were executed in the Town Mor for wiches. Mathew Boumer, Isabell Brown, Margrit Maddeson, Ann Watson, Ellenor Henderson, Ellenor Rogers, Elsabeth Dobson, Mrs. Ellsabeth Anderson, Jane Hunter, Jane Koupling, Margrit Brown, Margrit Moffit, Kattren Welsh, Aylles Hume, and Marie Pootes.' On the

---

[1] 5 Eliz. c. 20.
[2] 23 Geo. III. c. 51.

same day were hanged nine thieves, and also ' Jane Martin for a wich, the myllers wif of Chattim.'

This entry refers to one of the blackest pages in the annals of British superstition. The inhabitants of Newcastle were in 1649 seized with a panic about witches,[1] and petitioned the Town Council that all suspected persons might be brought to trial. The magistrates accordingly sent to Scotland for a ' witch-tryer,' who pretended to have special gifts of discerning those who had sold themselves to the devil, and they promised him 20s. for every witch he could convict. On his arrival, the public bellman was sent through the town ' ringing his bell and crying, that any woman complained against for a witch should be forthwith sent for, and tried by the person appointed.' Thirty women were accordingly brought into the Town Hall, and stripped, when the witch-tryer openly thrust pins into the tender parts of their bodies to test their sensibility. Most of them were found guilty, but only sixteen survived their tortures to die on the gallows. The accounts [2] of the Corporation, 1650, contain these items :

' Paid to the constables for carrying the witches to gaol, 4s. ; a grave for a witch, 6d. ; for trying the witches, 1l. 5s.'

Witchcraft was an offence against the Church, which was not directly punishable by the civil power before the change of religion in England. The first penal statute[3] against witches was enacted in 1541, when Cranmer enjoined his clergy

' to seek for any that use charms, sorcery, enchantments, witchcraft, soothsaying, or any like craft invented by the devil.'

But few executions took place under this law, which was repealed in the next reign, as savouring of Popery, and no fresh law was made until 1563,[4] when public opinion was exasperated by Bishop Jewell's preaching before Queen Elizabeth on the wickedness and danger of disobeying the Scriptural precept to put witches to death.[5] This sermon made the deeper impression on the Queen, because current rumour confidently attributed the early death of Charles IX. of France to the grievous sin which he had committed in sparing the life of the famous sorcerer Trois Echelles, and in the following year a new law of increased severity was made, which was rigidly enforced.[6] James I. was a firm believer in Satanic agency, and presided in person at the trial of Dr. Finn, who was tortured into confessing that

---

[1] Brand's *Hist. of Newcastle*, 4to. vol. ii. p. 477. Gardner's *England's Grievance*, 1655, p. 106. Whitelock's *Memorials*, p. 418.
[2] *Life of Mr. Barnes.* [3] 33 Hen. VIII. cap. 8. [4] 5 Eliz. cap. 16.
[5] Jewell's *Sermons*, Parker Society, p. 1028.
[6] Strype's *Annals of the Reformation*, vol. i. p. 11.

he had, in league with the devil, aroused the storm which obstructed the King's return from Denmark.[1]

The first Parliament of this reign declared witchcraft felony without benefit of clergy, which subjected witches to the penalty of death on the first conviction.[2] Amongst the innocent victims of this cruel statute were nine wretched women, who were executed at Leicester on July 18, 1616, for bewitching the son of Mr. Smith, of Husband's Bosworth, the brother of Henry Smith, the *silver-tongued preacher*.[3] Their execution was a disgrace to Sir Humphrey Winch, the judge who presided at the trial, for when King James visited Leicester a month afterwards he discovered by a personal examination of the boy, that an imposture had been practised, and that the women had been falsely accused.[4]

Public opinion in the next generation was predisposed by Puritanical teaching to see Satanic influence everywhere at work, and fanatics were firmly persuaded that it was a Christian duty to extirpate witches without mercy. There is reason to believe that during the few years of the Commonwealth more witches perished judicially in England than in the whole period before or after.[5] In Suffolk alone sixty persons were hung for witchcraft in a single year. That county was pronounced by Matthew Hopkins, the famous witch-finder, to be infested with witches, and accordingly it was visited by a Parliamentary Commission, to which two distinguished Presbyterian divines were attached as assessors.

> ' Hath not this present Parliament
> A ledger to the devil sent,
> Fully empowered to treat about
> Finding revolted witches out ?
> And has not he within a year
> Hanged threescore of them in one shire ' ? [6]

This morbid fear of witches at this period was pre-eminently a Protestant[7] superstition, which men of known piety and genius shared with the vulgar. That humane judge, Sir Matthew Hale, directed the jury in 1664 to convict two women tried before him for witchcraft, and felt no scruples in leaving them for execution ; [8] whilst Sir Thomas Browne, who was not only the ingenious writer against *vulgar errors*, but also a great

---

[1] Pitcairn's *Criminal Trials of Scotland,* vol. i. part ii. p. 213.
[2] 1 Jac. I. c. 12.
[3] Nichols's *Hist. of Leicestershire,* quoted in *Annual Register* 1800.
[4] Foss's *Biographia Juridica,* p. 748.
[5] Lecky's *Rationalism,* vol. i. p. 107.
[6] *Hudibras,* part ii. canto iii.
[7] Aikin's *Memoirs of Huet, Bp. of Avranches,* vol. ii. p. 397.
[8] *Collection of Curious Tracts relating to Witchcraft,* London, 1838.

physician, appeared as a witness at the trial and swore to their guilt. The same writer asserts in his *Religio Medici*[1] that those who deny the existence of witches are 'a sort not of Infidels but of Atheists.' The pious Baxter, too, positively ex-ulted in the legal murder of a poor old crazed vicar, nearly eighty years of age, who, after being a minister without reproach for fifty years, was accused of dealings with the devil. Before the poor old man was hanged, they extorted from him a confession too absurd for belief, which Baxter[2] gravely reproduces 'for the conversion of the Sadducee and the Infidel.'

'Among the rest, an *old reading parson* named Lewis, not far from Framlingham, was one that was hanged, who confessed that he had two imps, and that one of them was always putting him on doing mischief, and (being near the sea) as he saw a ship under sail, it moved him to send him to sink the ship, and he consented, and saw the ship sink before him.'

Baxter's writings were eagerly read on the other side of the Atlantic, and the authority of his great name encouraged the Puritan clergy in America in prosecutions as cruel as the Spanish Inquisition ever attempted in its worst days. When an old man of eighty was judicially pressed to death for refusing to plead to a charge of witchcraft, the ministers of Boston and Charleston united in an address thanking the Commissioners for their zeal[3] and entreating them to persevere.

After the Revolution of 1688 the superstition steadily lost ground in England, but there is evidence, that down to the end of the seventeenth century men were believed to die from being bewitched, and that an old woman, who was suspected of being a witch, could be persecuted to death with impunity.

HOLY ISLAND, NORTHUMBERLAND. '1691. William Cleugh be-*witched to death*; buried 16 July.'

COGGESHALL, ESSEX. '1699, Dec. 27. The widow Comon, that was counted a witch, was buried.'

The rude trials which this poor creature had undergone are described in the following extracts from Archdeacon Bufton's diary:[4]

'1699, July 13. The widow Comon was put into the river to see if she would sink, because she was suspected to be a witch, and she did not sink, but swim.

'July 19. She was tried again by putting her into the river, and she swam again.

---

[1] Browne's *Religio Medici*, 1672, p. 24.
[2] Baxter's *Certainty of the World of Spirits*, 1691, p. 53.
[3] Bancroft's *Hist. of the United States*, ch. xix.
[4] *Essex Archæologia*, vol. i. p. 126.

' July 24. She was tried a third time, and she swam and did not sink.'

The eighteenth century was more sceptical, and the growth of disbelief was unmistakably shown in 1712, when Jane Wenham was convicted of conversing with the devil in the shape of a cat, by a Hertfordshire jury against the express direction of the presiding judge.[1] Judge Powell ridiculed the accusation, and by his exertions the sentence was remitted, although the clergy who had taken part in the prosecution joined in a solemn protest, ending ' *liberavimus animas nostras.*' Unhappily, however, all the judges were not equally enlightened, and Mrs. Hicks and her daughter,[1] a child of nine, were hanged at Huntingdon on July 28, 1716, for raising a storm of wind by pulling off their stockings and making a lather of soap in a basin in league with the devil ! This was the last execution of its kind in England, and the superstition died out so rapidly amongst educated persons that the laws against witches were repealed in 1736 with little opposition.

From the time that it ceased to be a legal offence to be a witch, suspected persons were entitled to protection, but ignorant fanaticism set the law at defiance, and on July 22, 1760, two men were sentenced at the Leicestershire Quarter Sessions to stand in the pillory and to lie in gaol for a month, for ducking some poor old women to see if they were witches.[2] The popular delusion, however, at this period, was still so strong, that many accused persons felt themselves compelled by public opinion to clear their characters by a voluntary submission to the accepted tests of guilt. One of the approved tests to discover a witch was to weigh the accused publicly in the scales against the Church Bible. Susanna Hammokes, an elderly married woman, at Wingrove near Ailesbury, was accused in 1759 by a neighbour of bewitching her spinning-wheel, so that she could not make it go round. The accuser offered to make oath of the fact before a magistrate, whereupon the husband of the accused insisted on vindicating his wife's character by a trial by the Church Bible. Accordingly, Mrs. Hammokes was on Feb. 25, 1759, solemnly conducted to the Parish Church, where she was stripped of all her clothes to her shift, and weighed against the great parish Bible, in the presence of all her neighbours. The result was, that to the no small mortification of her accuser, she outweighed the Bible, and was triumphantly acquitted of the charge.[3] Another infallible test was to be ducked in a pond; for it was firmly believed that the devil

[1] *Blackwood's Magazine*, May 1859.
[2] *Annual Register*, 1760, vol. iii. p. 113.
[3] *Ibid.* 1759, vol. ii. p. 73.

would never allow his votaries to be drowned. In July 1760, two old women at Glen, in Leicestershire, challenged each other to submit to this test. They both accepted the ordeal, and after being stripped to their shifts, had their thumbs and great toes tied across them, when they were hauled, each with a cart-rope round her waist, into a gravel pit, full of water, to see if they would swim. One of them sank at once, and was acquitted. The other succeeded in struggling up to the surface, and was forced to confess herself guilty.[1] The credulity, however, of the vulgar is less to be wondered at, than that, in 1768, when educated Englishmen were agreed in the conviction that witch-craft was a delusion, John Wesley should deliberately write in his journal,

' The giving up witchcraft is in effect giving up the Bible.'

HARTLEPOOL. ' 1673, 5 Oct. Tho. Smailes was buryed and crowned by a jury of 12 men, and John Harrison supposed to murder him.'

NEWINGTON BUTTS. ' 1689. John Arris and Derwick Farlin in one grave, being both Dutch soldiers ; one killed the other drinking brandy, buried Nov. 1.'

TEDDINGTON, MIDDLESEX. ' 1743–4. James Parsons, who had often eat a shoulder of mutton or a peck of hasty pudding at a time, which caused his death, was buried 7 March, aged 36.'

Sometimes the occupation and quality of the deceased is recorded : thus,

LANDBEACH, CAMBS. ' 1538, 2 Nov. Mr. James Hutton *Pryst* depted unto God.'

ST. BENET FINK, LONDON. ' 1542. Thomas Pickerell, a *beadsman of St. Anthony's*, bur. 5 May.'

STREATHAM. ' 1548. Rich d Adams *the hermite*, bur. 29 Apr.'

ST. GILES, CRIPPLEGATE. ' 1569. Ails Walsay, a *nonne*, was buried 3rd June.'

LEOMINSTER, CO. HEREFORD. ' 1577. Dnus Bell, Capitalis Baro Scaccarii Angliæ, sepultus fuit XXV° die Julii.'

Sir Robert Bell, Lord Chief Baron of the Exchequer, died on circuit at Leominster from the effects of gaol fever, which he had caught at the Oxford Summer Assizes, long remembered as the ' *Black Assize.*'[2] The weather was sultry, and the Court-house was crowded to suffocation on July 6, 1577, when Rowland Jenks, the stationer, was condemned to have his ears cropped off for sedition. The prisoner was no sooner removed after sentence, than a blast of fœtid air from the dungeons beneath poisoned the Court, and infected all who were present. Above

---

[1] *Annual Register*, 1760, vol. iii. p. 320.
[2] Hollinshed, vol. iii. p. 1270.

600 persons sickened in one day, and 510 died within the next five weeks. The two judges, five of the magistrates, and most of the jury were amongst the victims, many of whom 'bled till they expired.' The news of this calamity was spread far and wide by a doleful ditty, in which Death enumerates its ghastly triumphs in these dogged lines.[1]

> Thinke you on the solemne Sizes past
> How sodenly in Oxfordshire
> I came and made the judges all agast,
>   And justices that did appear;
> And tooke both Bell and Barham away,
> And many a worthy man that day,
> And all their bodies brought to clay.'

Such visitations, however, were not infrequent as long as the gaols were hotbeds of fever from dirt and want of ventilation. At the Lent Assizes for Devon, in 1585, the Recorder, eleven of the jury, and six county magistrates sickened and died of a putrid fever, which the prisoners at the bar brought from Exeter gaol.[2] But notwithstanding this warning, the contemporary narrative of the Jesuit, F. Henry More, gives a frightful description of Exeter Castle in 1604, when F. Laithwaite, the Jesuit, was confined there for refusing to take the oath of supremacy. Eighty men and women were huddled together in one filthy dungeon, where they were all chained by the feet to an iron ring in such a manner that they could only just change their position by sitting standing or lying down. They were eaten up by vermin, and surrounded by filth, which they had no means of removing, and the Jesuit's hands feet and face were so much swollen that he could not sleep for pain, whilst the stench made food loathsome.[3] The prisoners fared no better in the Gatehouse at Westminster, where Robert Southwell, the Jesuit, was confined in 1592; for his father, a favourite at Court, who had married a relation of Queen Elizabeth's, found his son

' covered with filth, swarming with vermin, with maggots crawling in his sores, his face blistered, and his bones almost protruding through his skin from want of food and nourishment.'[4]

The state of English prisons continued to be a disgrace to humanity until the middle of the last century; and although Howard's benevolent exertions were not without some effect on public opinion, no effectual attempt was made to improve the

---

[1] Plot's *Natural History of Oxfordshire*, p. 8. Anthony Wood's *Annals of Oxford*, July 1577.
[2] Oliver's *Hist. of Exeter*, 8vo. 1861, p. 191.
[3] F. Henry More's *History of the English Province*.
[4] Foley's *Records of the English Jesuits*.

sanitary arrangements of gaols until 1749, when Mr. Fox, who was then Sècretary-at-War, was induced to authorise the experiment of ventilating the Savoy prison. Ventilators accordingly were fixed in 1749, and the putrid air was so effectually expelled, that whereas in previous years the prisoners died of gaol fever, fifty and a hundred at a time, there was not a single death from this cause for three years after the prison was ventilated.[1] In the meantime the City authorities remained passive, until in 1750 they were startled out of their apathy by a catastrophe, which drew public attention to the state of Newgate. The Sessions of the Old Bailey were held in a room about thirty feet square, which was unusually crowded on May 11, 1750, to hear the trial of Captain Clarke for the murder of Captain Innes. Adjoining the Court were two small rooms about twelve feet square, and only seven feet high, in which more than 100 prisoners were huddled together during the Sessions, waiting their trials. These dens had not been properly cleansed for years, and no attempt was made to purify and disinfect the prisoners when they were brought up for trial from their filthy cells in Newgate ; the result was, that the crowd in Court was poisoned by the stench and foul air, and a malignant fever broke out, which carried off no less than forty persons within a fortnight. Amongst the victims were two of the judges, Sir Thomas Abney and Baron Garrow, one of the Sheriffs and Sir Daniel Lambert, an Alderman and ex-Lord Mayor. Public opinion was shocked, and it was ordered that in future the Court of the Old Bailey and the gaol of Newgate be thoroughly drenched with vinegar before the Sessions, and that the prisoners be washed with the same disinfectant before they were brought into Court, whilst the number brought up at any one time was never to exceed fifteen. Nothing, however, was done for the ventilation of Newgate, and the air of the prison was so foul that some workmen employed there in July 1752 were attacked by gaol fever, which they carried home to their families with fatal result.[2]

ST. ANNE'S, BLACKFRIARS. ' 1580. William, *foole* to my Lady Jerningham, bur. 21 March.'

ST. JOHN'S, NEWCASTLE-ON-TYNE. ' 1589. Edward Errington, the *Towne's Fooll,* bur. 23 Aug., died in the peste.'

CHESTER-LE-STREET. ' 1627. Ellis Thompson, *insipiens,* Gul. Lambton Militis, bur. 26 Apr.'

' Fools ' were privileged domestics in great households until the Civil Wars, when they were generally discarded. Thomas

---

[1] *Gent. Mag.* 1753, vol. xxiii. p. 71.
[2] *Gent. Mag.* vol. xx. p. 235, and vol. xxiii. p. 21. *Middlesex Archæol. Society's Transactions,* vol. iii. p. 467.

Williams, 'a pleasant fool' of Earl Coningsby's, who died in 1687, is reputed to have been the last of them. His portrait is still to be seen at Hampton Court,[1] in Herefordshire, which was formerly the seat of the Coningsbys.

ST. NICOLAS, DURHAM. '1620. John Haward, *Saltpetreman*, bur. 9 Sept.'

Before the discovery and importation of Indian nitre, saltpetre was manufactured from earth impregnated with animal matter, and being the chief ingredient of gunpowder, was claimed in most countries as a State monopoly. Patents for making saltpetre were expressly exempted in 1624 from the statute against monopolies,[2] and the saltpetreman was empowered to break open all premises, and to dig up the floors of stables and even dwelling-houses. This privilege was so unscrupulously exercised, that we read in Archbishop Laud's Diary (1624, Dec. 13), that the 'saltpeterman had digged in the colledge church of Brecknock for his work, bearing too bold upon his commission.' Charles I., in 1625 and again in 1634, commanded by proclamation,[3] that no dovehouse or stable should be paved, but should lie open for the growth of saltpetre, and that none should presume to hinder any saltpetreman from digging where he thought proper. The vexation and oppression of the king's subjects by the saltpetremen is specially mentioned in the famous 'Remonstrance[4] of the State of the Kingdom' in 1641; but no effectual remedy was applied until 1656,[5] when it was enacted that no saltpetreman should dig within any houses or lands without previously obtaining the leave of the owner. This vexatious prerogative of the Crown was maintained in France until 1778, and was not abolished in Prussia until 1798.[6]

ST. GILES, CRIPPLEGATE. '1607. The dau. of Richard Michell, *aquavity-man*, bur. 8 June.'

ST. NICHOLAS, NEWCASTLE-ON-TYNE. '1627. Margret the *Grace wyfe*[7] (grosse femme), bur. 11 June.'

DURHAM CATHEDRAL. '1627. Robert Grinwell, *lutenist*, bur. 12 April.'

BLICKLING, NORFOLK. '1627-8. Robert Linning, ye architect builder of Blickling Hall, buried 8 Jan.'

The name of the architect of this noble pile of buildings, which is one of the finest specimens in England of the Jacobian style, has been preserved by the accident of his death before

[1] *Gent. Mag.* July 1825.   [2] 21 Jac. I. c. 3, s. 10.
[3] *Notes and Queries,* vol. vii. p. 433.
[4] *Parl. Hist.* vol. ii. p. 950.
[5] *Scobell,* p. 377.
[6] Beckman's *Hist. of Inventions,* ed. Bohn, vol. ii. p. 511.
[7] Mr. Burn (p. 127) misreads it ' *grave* wife.'

the completion of the fabric. The Hall was commenced by Sir Henry Hobart, Lord Chief Justice of Common Pleas, who died on December 29, 1625, for it is recorded in the parish register that Paul Stone, 'a stranger coming to work at the building of the Hall,' was buried at Blickling on June 20, 1624. ·This date is fatal to the local tradition, that the ill-fated Queen Anne Boleyne was born in one of the chambers of this mansion. Blickling was for some generations the seat of the Boleynes, and on their extinction was inherited by the Cleres of Ormesby, who were descended from Alice Boleyne, the aunt of Queen Anne Boleyne. Sir Edward Clere sold the manor in Michaelmas Term, 1616, subject to the life interest of his stepmother, Dame Frances Clere, to Sir Henry Hobart, who compounded with the dowager for immediate possession by an annuity of £400 a year during her life. His son and heir, Sir John Hobart, completed the Hall as it now stands.

STEPNEY. ' 1628. William, a dumb man, who died in Ratcliffe Highway, a *fortune-teller*, bur. 24 Sept.'

HACKNEY, MIDDLESEX. ' 1628. Mountagu Wood, a *nurse child*, buried 6 October.'

It was the fashion at this period for Londoners of condition to place their infant children out at nurse in ·the suburbs, and it was one of the oratorical triumphs of Henry Smith, the Silver-tongued Preacher, that by the force of his eloquence 'many persons of honour and worship, ladies and great gentlewomen, were persuaded to recall their children home forthwith, and to suckle them themselves.' Sir William Herrick, who was Queen Elizabeth's Ambassador to the Sublime Porte, and held several lucrative places in the Exchequer, records in his Diary the different suburbs of London where his eight children were nursed, and how much he paid for each of them :

'My son Thomas (born 3 May, 1602) was "nursed at Petersham at two shillings a week, lived not long, but died there at nurse, and was buried in the Church there." '

'Elizabeth (born 6 May, 1603) was "nursed at Highgate at 2/6 a week, but lived above a year, and died there, and was buried at St. Pankers Church in the Fields by my cozen Toby." '

BASSINGBOURN, CAMBS. '1654. Mr. Kettle, the *King's falkner*, bur. 5 June.'

BARWELL, CO. LEIC. '1655. Mr. Gregory Isham, *attorney and husbandman*, bur. 7 Oct.' [1]

NORBOROUGH, CO. NORTHAMPTON. '1665. Elizabeth, the relict of Oliver Cromwell, sometime Pro : of England, was buried Nov. 19.' She died at the house of her son-in-law, John Cleypole,

---

[1] Nichols's *Hist. of co. Leicester*, vol. iii. p. 156.

Esq., of Norborough, who was Master of the Horse to the Protector, and a Member of his House of Lords. His mutilation of the parish register of Norborough, from which the entries from 1613 to 1646 have been torn out, is recorded in the following memorandum:

'The reason of this defect in the register was because one Mr. John Cleypole, *a factious gentleman*, then living in the parish of Northborough, caused the register to be taken away from mee, JOHN STOUGHTON, then Rector, for which I was by the Ecclesiastical Court then holden at St. Martin's adjudged for satisfaction the sum of £2. 10s., which was paid me at the charge of the parish by Robert Cooke, then churchwarden. JOHANNES STOUGHTON.' [1]

BUXTED, SUSSEX. '1666. Richard Bassett the old clarke of this Parish who had continued in the offices of clarke and Sexton for the space of 43 years, whose melody warbled forth as if he had been thumped on the back with a stone, was buried 20 Sept.'

WESTMINSTER ABBEY. 'Aug. 1666. Sir William *Bartly*, who died honorably in his Majesty's service at sea, and was imbalmed by the Hollanders (who had taken his body with the ship wherein he was slain), and sent over by them into England at the request and charges of his relations, was buried in the North aisle of the monuments, near the door opening thereto.'

Sir William Berkeley (whose name is here phonetically written Bartly), Vice-Admiral of the White, was the third son of Charles, second Viscount Fitzharding, and was slain in a sea fight with the Dutch on June 3, 1666, whilst commanding his own ship, *The Swiftsure*. He was only twenty-seven years of age, and his gallantry made such an impression on the Dutch, that his imbalmed corpse was deposited in state in the great church at the Hague, until it was sent to England by a special messenger. The spelling of this entry proves that the present pronunciation of the family name is more than two centuries old.

BRIGNAL, YORKSHIRE. '1674. Alexander Willis, caucianus, dum forte *calographiam hic docuit*, variolis correptus mortem obiit.'

CAMBERWELL. '1687. Robert Hern and Elizabeth Bozwell, *King and Queen of the Gipsies*, bur. 2 June.'

ST. ANDREW'S, NEWCASTLE-ON-TYNE. '1697. Mary, dau. of James Brown, *lume sweeper* (chimney sweeper), bur. 13 May.'

HALLATON, CO. LEICESTER. '1700. John, son of William Dent, *gentile yeoman*, buried 7 Aug.'

ST. MARY-LE-BOW, DURHAM. '1722. Brian Pearson, the Abbey *dog whipper*, bur. 6 April.'

Payments 'for whipping dogs out of the church' constantly occur in churchwardens' accounts,[2] and the 'dog-noper,' an

---

[1] Bridges's *Hist. of Co. Northampton*, vol. ii. p. 531. Rev. John Stoughton was inducted Nov. 25, 1659, and died rector March 15, 1695-6.

[2] viij*d.* was the amount paid at Ludlow in 1543 and 1560. *Churchwardens Accounts*, Ludlow, 1540-74. Edited by T. Wright for the Camden Society, 1869.'

official appointed for this purpose, still holds office at[1] Ecclesfield. In the church of Northorpe, co. Lincoln,[2] there was until
about fifty years ago, a small pew called 'the hall dog-pew,' in
which the dogs which followed the squire to church were confined during Divine service.

The churchwardens of Trysull, in Staffordshire, still receive
an annuity of £1 a year under the Will of John Rudge, Esq.,
dated April 17, 1725.[3] He charged his lands for ever with the
payment of five shillings a quarter to a poor man, who was to
walk up and down the parish church during Divine service for
the double purpose of driving stray dogs out of the church and
waking up any of the congregation who went to sleep during
the sermon. A similar rentcharge of eight shillings a year is
paid at Claverley, in Shropshire, under a Deed dated August 23,
1659.[4]

St. Clement's, Hastings. '1758. John Jacob Sur *the linguist*,
belonging to Captain Greyling's privateer, bur. 31 May.'

Sproxton, co. Leic. '1768. A *Tom o' Bedlam*, bur. 22 Dec.'

Marske, Yorkshire. '1781. James Postlethwaite, the *Popish
priest* at Clintz, buried 10 Feb. "The service by request was read
as usual."'

Totteridge, Herts. '1802, March 2. Buried Elizabeth King,
widow, for 46 years clerk of this parish, in the 91st year of her
age, who died at Whetstone, in the Parish of Finchley, Feb. 24th.
N.B. This old woman, as long as she was able to attend, did constantly, and read on the prayer days, with great strength and
pleasure to the hearers, though not in the clerk's place; the desk
being filled on the Sunday by her son-in-law Benjamin Withall, who
did his best.'

Christian burial in consecrated places was sternly denied to
suicides and Anabaptists, and even Catholics were treated as
dying excommunicated in the reign of Queen Elizabeth.

St. Anne's, Blackfriars, London. '1579, Aug. 4. John hacone
infamously buried, for killing himself desperately.'

Barking. '1593. June 15. Alice, the wife of John But, Gent.
Consulto prius Episcopo num omnino sepeliretur, quia Cacolicæ
(sic) relligionis mortis tempore fautrix et amica fuit, ideoque ex-
communicata in cœmiterio jacet.'

Christ Church, Hants. '1604, April 14. Christian Steevens,
the wife of Thomas Steevens, died in childbirth, and was buried
by women, for she was a papishe.'

Weedon Beck, Northamptonshire. '1615. William Radhouse
the elder, dying excommunicated, was buried by stealth in the

---

[1] Eastwood's *Hist. of Ecclesfield*, p. 219.
[2] *Archæologia*, vol. xli. p. 365, *note.*
[3] *Charity Commission Reports*, vol. iv. p. 248.
[4] *Idem*, vol. v. p. 634.

night time in the churchyard, 29 Jan.; whereupon the church was interdicted a fortnight.'

An interdicted church had to be 'new hallowed' by a solemn service; and when St. Mary's, Cambridge, was interdicted for the burial of Mr. Bucer, the churchwarden's accounts contained these charges,

'Paid for frankincense and sweet perfumes for the sacrament and herbs used at the new hallowing.'

STOCK HARWARD, ESSEX. '1642. Elizabeth, the daughter of Thomas Wood (an Anabaptisticall and factious separatist), and Eleanor his wife (the grave being ready made), was (by the companie that came with the child) interred and laid into the ground before the minister came, and without praires, or the right to Christian burial according to the order of the Church of England on Satterday.' May 7.

TODDINGTON, BEDS. '1658. Thomas Matthew died the 12th day of November, and was buried the 14th day of November, 1658, in his garden, late taken out of his orchard.'

'1663, Oct. 8. Anne White, widow, buried in the Quakers' burying-place by Edmund White, yᵉ Anabaptist, contrary to law.'

KNIPTON, co. LEICESTER. '1665, March 11. Cecily Grosse, an Anabaptist, the wife of J. Grosse, oatmealman, was *Anabaptistically buried.*'

WARLEGGAN, CORNWALL. '1681. George Piper, an Anabaptist, tumbled in ye ground Feb. 25.'

TODDINGTON, BEDS. '1725, March 21. Bernard Stoniford, bricklayer, hurled into a grave.'

'1728, Aug. 26. Mary Shaw, widow, hurled into yᵉ ground.'

The present statutory entries of baptism and burial are too well known to be extracted here. They have the merit of uniformity, and of supplying better evidence to determine the identity of the parties. But uniformity has the defect that it excludes zeal and industry, as well as negligence; and future antiquaries will miss with regret those illustrations of local history and contemporary manners, which enlivened the register when it was left to the Parson's discretion to insert what he thought fit. So far from being under any obligation to keep a mere dry record of dates and names, the Parson was encouraged by his Bishop to take pride in making his parish register a *Chronicon mirabile*. That learned prelate, Dr. White Kennett, Bishop of Peterborough (1718–28), took occasion in his charge at his first visitation to say to his clergy:

'One thing more I would intimate to you, that you are not only obliged to enter the day and year of every christening, wedding, or burial, but it is left to your discretion to enter down any notable incident of times and seasons, especially relating to your own parish, and the neighbourhood of it, such as storms and lightning, contagion, and mortality, drought, scarcity, plenty, longevity, robbery, murders, or the like casualties. If such memorable things were fairly entered, your parish registers would become chronicles of many strange occurrences that would not otherwise be known, and would be of great use and service for posterity to know. You have had precedents of this kind in parochial registers within this diocese, and they have been cited to very good purpose by our worthy brother (Dr. T. Morton), the author of *the Natural History of this county of Northampton.*'[1]

Precedents can be found in different registers of all the subjects enumerated by the Bishop; and I have selected, as examples, entries of the great snow of 1615, and the drought which followed it, of the scarcity of 1587 and 1621, of the plenty of 1620, the frost of 1684, and the storm of 1703.

YOULGRAVE, DERBYSHIRE. '1614–15. Jan. 16, began the greatest snow which ever fell upon the earth, within man's memorye. It cover'd the earth fyve quarters deep upon the playne. And for heapes or drifts of snow, they were very deep, so that passengers, both horse and foot, passed over gates, hedges and walls. It fell at ten several times, and the last was the greatest, to the greate admiration and feare of all the land, for it came from the foure p^{ts} of the world, so that all c'ntryes were full, yea, the south p'te as well as these mountaynes. It continued by daily encreasing untill the 12th day of March (without the sight of any earth eyther uppon hilles or valleyes), upon wch daye, beinge the Lordes day, it began to decrease; and so by little and little consumed and wasted away, till the 28th day of May, for then all the heapes or drifts of snow were consumed, except one uppon Kinder-Scout, wch lay till Witson week.'

' *The name of our Lord be praysed.*'

' There fell also ten lesse snowes in Aprill, some a foote deep, some lesse, but none continued long. Uppon Mayday, in the morning, instead of fetching in flowers, the youths brought in flakes of snow, which lay above a foot deep uppon the moores and mountayns.'

The great snow was followed by a drought.

' 1615. There was no rayne fell upon the earth from the 25th day of March till the 2nd day of May, & then there was but one shower, after which there fell none tyll the 18th day of June, & then there fell another; after y^t there fell none at all till the 4th day of August, after which tyme there was sufficient rayne uppon the earth; so that the greatest p^t of this land, especially the south p^{ts} were burnt upp both corne and hay. An ordinary sumer load of hay was at £2, and little or none to be gott for money. This p^t

---

[1] Lansdowne MS. in Brit. Museum, No. 957.

of the peake was very sore burnt upp, onely Lankishyre and Cheshyre had rayne ynough all sumer; and both corne and hay sufficient. There was very little rayne fell the last winter, but snowe onely.'

St. Oswald's, Durham. '1587. Thys yere the pryce of corne was as followeth, and y⁰ greatest part of last yeare beforegoinge, so y⁴ many poore peple weare supposed to dye for lack of bredde, notwithstandyng greate store in the handes of hard harted carles, y⁴ styll raysed the p'ce untyll harvest, at the which tyme y⁰ price of corne begane to fall. The p'ce of Rye xiij*s*. iiij*d*. the bushell, Wheat at xvj*s*. iiij*d*. the b'shell, Pese at xij*s*. y⁰ bushell; but the next somer Wheat was at iij*s*. iv*d*. the bushell, Rye and Pays at iiij*s*. y⁰ bushell.'

Isham, Northamptonshire. '1620. This was a cheap yeare of all grain. Ordinary Wheat at 18*s*. the stryke; Rye at 16*s*., and after at 12*s*.; Barley at 9*s*. 10*d*., and Mault at 15*s*. a stryke.'

'1621. A very dear yeare of all manner of corne, and about the end of 1622, Wheat 4*s*. and more the bushel; Barley 3*s*.; Mault 4*s*., and the prices of all these some market-days more.'

Holy-rood Church, Southampton. '1683–4. This yeare was a great Frost, which began before Christmasse, soe that y⁰ 3rd and 4th dayes of this month of February y⁰ River of Southampton was frossen all over and covered with ice from Calshott Castle to Redbridge, and Tho: Martaine ma^r of a vessell went upon y⁰ ice from Berry near Marchwood to Milbrook-point. And y⁰ river at Ichen Ferry was so frossen over that severall persons went from Beauvois-hill to Bittern Farme forwards and backwards.'

The frost lasted eight weeks, and the fair held on the Thames, during its continuance, is described with many interesting details in the *Diaries* of Luttrell and Evelyn. The Thames has been four times since that date sufficiently frozen to hold a fair on; viz. in 1716, in 1740, in 1789, and in 1814. In 1740 tents on the ice were inhabited for weeks, and there are many still living who remember the merriment of the Frost Fair of 1814.

St. Oswald's, Durham. '1703. Mem., that on y⁰ 27th Nov. was y⁰ greatest hurricane & storme that ever was knowne in England: many churches and houses were extreamely shattered, and thousands of trees blown down; 13 or more of her Maj'tyes men of war were cast away, and above 2,000 seamen perished in them. N.B.—The storme came no further north than Yarmouth.'

This is the storm to which Addison alludes in his famous comparison of Marlborough on the battle-field of Blenheim to an angel guiding the whirlwind.[1] No such tempest was ever known in our latitude. It was long remembered as a national calamity, and was the occasion of a public fast, which was solemnly kept by the Queen's proclamation on January 19, 1704.[2] Amongst

[1] Macaulay's *Essay on Addison.*
[2] Stanhope's *Hist. of England*, pp. 104–8.

other lives which were lost, the Bishop of Bath and Wells was killed in his bed, and his palace was blown down.

The registers abound with details of those fearful epidemics which devastated England at recurring intervals in the sixteenth and seventeenth centuries. I begin with notices of the *sweating sickness* of 1551, which Dr. Caius, in his 'boke[1] or counseill against the sweate,' reckons as the 'fifth visitation of this fearful Ephemera of Englande.'

LOUGHBOROUGH, CO. LEIC. '1551. The swat called *New acquaintance,* alias *Stoupe Knave and know thy Master,* began 24 June.' Hancock says in his Autobiography:[2]

'God plaged thys realme most justly for our sinns with three notable plages: The first was the posting swet, that posted from towne to towne throughe England, and was named *stope gallant,* for hytt spared none, for ther were dawncyng in the cowrte at 9 a'clocke thatt were deadd or eleven a'clocke. In the same swett also at Cambredge[3] died too worthy impes, the dewke of Swffok hys son Charells, and hys brother.'

'The *stup-gallant* or the *hote sickness*' is also mentioned in the registers of Uffcolme,[4] Devon, in August, 1551. This quaint name was taken from the French, for the epidemic which ravaged France in 1528 was called[5] the '*trousse gallant,*' because it chiefly attacked young men in full health and strength. In the same grotesque spirit the plague of 1675 was called[6] '*the jolly rant*' at Newcastle-on-Tyne.

The sweating sickness was succeeded by the plague, which made its first appearance in England in 1591, and was brought to London in some bales of cloth imported from the Levant. The infection was soon carried into the provinces, and amongst other towns Derby suffered terribly in 1592.

ST. ALKMOND'S, DERBY. '1592, October. Hic incipit pestis pestifera.'

The visitation lasted twelve months; and although there were not two houses together free from it, it never entered the house of a tanner, a tobacconist, or a shoemaker. Whilst it lasted, a small basin of vinegar was placed on a stone on the four steps known as the Headless Cross. The country people brought their provisions to market at this spot, where they stood with

---

[1] Reprinted in the Appendix to Hecker's *Epidemics of the Middle Ages.* Sydenham Society, 1844.
[2] *Narratives of the Reformation,* p. 82. Camden Society 1859.
[3] The Dukes did not die at Cambridge, but at Buckden Palace, Hunts, on July 16, 1551. Cooper's *Athenæ Cant.* i. 105.
[4] Lyson's *Magna Britannia,* Devon.
[5] *Hecker,* p. 235.
[6] *Brand,* vol. ii. p. 494.

their mouths filled with tobacco, and the purchasers put their
money into the basin. It appears from another register in the
same town, that the plague ceased as suddenly as it began.

ALL SAINTS, DERBY. ' October, 1593. About this time the plague
of pestilence by the great mercy and goodness of God stayed, past
all expectation of man, for it ceased upon a sodayne, at whych
tyme it was dispersed in every corner of this whole parish; there
was not two houses together free from it, and yet the Lord bade
the Angel stay, as in David's tyme, hys name be blessed for that.'
EDWARD BENNETT, *Minister.*

From this time until after the Great Fire of 1666, London
was subjected from time to time to renewals of the plague;
and our knowledge of the severity of the visitation in different
parts of England in the years 1604, 1606, 1625, 1630, and
1665, is mainly derived from parish registers.

ST. GILES, DURHAM. ' 1604. Ann Ourd, wyffe of Christopher
Ourd, bur. 25 Jan. So all the hole household dyed in the vicitacion
at this time, and so y° plague ceased.'

PETERBOROUGH. ' 1606, Dec. 16. Henry Renoulds was buryed.'
' Henry came from London where he dwelt, sicke of the plague,
& being receyved by William Browne, died in his house. The
said William soon after fell sicke of the plague and died, so did his
sonne, his daughter, and his servant; only his wyfe and her mayde
escaped with soars. The plague brought by this means to Peter-
burgh continued there till September following.'

LITTLE MARLOW, BUCKS. ' 1625, July 18. Mary,· wife of Sir
William Borlase, a gratious ladye she was, dyed of the plague, as
did 18 more.'

The horrible desolation described in the next series of extracts
can scarcely be surpassed, when we find a plague-stricken
patient digging his own grave and laying himself in it, under
the conviction that the survivors of his family will be physically
unable to bury him.

MALPAS, CHESHIRE.[1] ' 1625, Aug. 13. Thomas Dawson of
Bradley, Thomas Jefferies his servant, and Richard Dawson his
son, were buried in the night. Ralph Dawson, another son of
Thomas, came from London about the 25th of July last past, &
being sick of the plague died in his father's house, and infected
the said house, and was buried, as was reported, neare unto his
father's house.'

' Aug. 15. Thomas Dawson was buried at 3 A.M.'

' August 20. Elizabeth Dawson his daughter, and Anne Dawson
his wife, were buried the same day.'

' Aug. 24. Richard Dawson, brother to the above-named
Thomas Dawson of Bradley, being sicke of the plague and per-
ceyveing he must die at y° time, arose out of his bed and made his

---

[1] Ormerod's *Hist. of Cheshire*, vol. ii. p. 332.

grave, and caused his nefew John Dawson to cast strawe into the grave, w'ch was not farre from the house, and went and lay'd him down in the say'd grave, and caused clothes to be layd uppon, and so dep'ted out of this world; this he did, because he was a strong man, and heavier than his said nefew and another wench were able to bury. He died about the xxivth of August. Thus much was I credibly tould he did.'

'Aug. 29. John Dawson, sonne of the above-mentioned Thomas, came unto his father when his father sent for him, being sicke, and haveyng layd him down in a dich, died in the night.'

'Sept. 15. Rose Smyth, servant of the above-named Thomas Dawson, and the last of yᵗ household, died of plague, and was buryed by Wm. Cooke near unto the saide hows.'

EGGLESCLIFF, CO. DURHAM. '1644. In this year there died of the plague in this town 21 people. They are not buried in the church-yard, and are not in the register.'

This omission is common enough at such periods, and at Ealing the field in which the victims of the plague were buried is still called ' *The Dead Man's Field.*'

RAMSEY, HUNTS. '1665, Feb. 400 people died of the plague.' The infection was brought from London in some cloth for a new coat. The gentleman who wore the coat was the first to sicken, and the tailor who made the coat died, with all his family.

Many trades no longer in use are noticed in registers :

ST. DUNSTAN'S WEST, LONDON.[1] '1591. Robert Dorrington, *spurrer.*'

'1592. John Fisher, *shiere-grinder.*'

'1597. A *comfit-maker.*'

'1601. Richard Delworth, *French-hood maker.*'

'1603. Dudley, son of Philip Rocetor, *musitioner.*'

'1603. Richard Oilworth, *tombmaker.*'

'1630. Daniel Hill, *panyerman* of the Middle Temple.' ' The panyer-man by the winding of his horn summons the gentlemen to dinner and supper.[2] He also provides mustard, pepper, and vinegar for the Hall.'

'1605. William Johnson, *wyredrawer.*'

'1605. Edmund Bedo, *tyremaker.*'

'1609. A *woodmonger.*'

'1603. Mr. Richard Deakes, *upholtster.*'

The fashion of duplicating the *er*, and of writing uphol-sterer, fruiterer, and poulterer, is modern. Poulter occurs in these registers in 1590, and is invariably so written in Stow's *Survey of London.*

---

[1] Nichols's *Collect. Top. and Gen.* vol. v. p. 378.
[2] Dugdale's *Orig. Jurid.* 1671, p. 200.

St. Peter's, Cheap, London. '1593. Joyce Hoode, mayden and *burnisher of plate,* buried.'

Marske, co. York. '1635. Ibbison, *a grove man* (a lead miner), buried.'

St. Nicholas, Newcastle-on-Tyne.[1] '1576. Robert Peacock, *sword-slipper.*'

'1582. Elias Partridge, *grate-maker*' (basket-maker).

'1588. Roland Hedley, *bowyer.*'

'1590. Robert Hedley, *fletcher.*'

'1595. Henry Gray, *furbisher.*'

'1602. Cornelius Branding, *pictor-maker.*'

'1661. Thomas Fletcher, *translatar*' (a species of cobbler).

All Saints, Newcastle-on-Tyne.[2] '1601. John Scott, *Jack-maker.*'

Stern discipline was enforced against offenders of all kinds in the days of Q. Elizabeth.

Kingston-on-Thames. '1572. On Tewsday being the xix. day of August. . . . Downinge wife to Downinge gravemaker of this parysshe, she was sett on a new *cukking stolle* made of a grett hythe, and so browght abowte the markett place to Temes brydge, and ther had iij Duckings over head and eres, becawse she was a common scolde and fyghter.'

This ʄucking-stool had just cost the parish '£1. 3*s.* 4*d.*, and was worked in a very ingenious manner. A post was firmly fixed in the bed of the river; on the top of the post was placed a transverse beam turning on a swivel, and the stool was attached to one end of it. When the culprit was tied to the stool, this end of the cross-beam was swung round towards the river, and let down into the water.'

A ducking-stool, a pillory, a cage, and stocks were the usual appendages to a manor, and were the signs of local jurisdiction. It is not so long ago that they have been disused in some places. The ducking-stool at Rugby was repaired at the expense of the parish in December 1741, and a man was ducked in it in 1786, for beating his wife, until he was half drowned. It was placed on the west side of a horse-pond near the path leading from the Clifton Road to the new churchyard.[3]

Kingston-on-Thames. '1572, Sept. 8. 'This day in this towne was kept the sessions of gayle Delyverye, and ther was hangid vj. persons, and xvij. taken for roges and vagabonds and whypped abowte the market place and brent in the ears.'

The parish priest was by vocation a peace-maker, and when

---

[1] Brand, vol. ii. pp. 360–2.
[2] *Surrey Archæologia,* vol. ii. 91.
[3] *Hist. of Rugby,* by N. H. Nicholas, 1826.

he made up quarrels between angry neighbours, the terms of reconciliation were often recorded in the parish register.

TWICKENHAM. '1568, Aprell 4. In the presence of the hole paryshe of Twycknam was agreement made betwyxt Mr. Parker & hys Wyffe and Hewe Rytte & Sicyly Daye of a slander brought up by the sayde Rytte and Sicyly Daye upon the aforesayde Mr. Parker.'

'1568, Aprell 10. Agreement was made between Thomas Whytt & James Herne, & have consented that whosoever geveth occasion of the breaking of Christen love and charyty betwyxt them, to ferfeit to the poor of the paryshe 3*s.* 4*d.*, being dewlye proved.'

The custom of recording such reconciliations in the parish books dates. from a very early period, for in 1363, when John de l'Isle, the grandson of Sir John de Bohun of Midhurst, the patron of Eastbourne Priory, made formal proof of his majority, one of the witnesses deposed that

' A great quarrel between John de l'Isle the father and Richard Broker was made up on the Sunday after the child was born, as it is *enrolled in the missal of Eastbourne Church.*'

The registers abound with examples of the severity with which the church in former times maintained its authority by compelling notorious delinquents to do public penance, and by excommunicating offenders against ecclesiastical discipline :—

CROYDON, SURREY.[1] ' 1597. Margaret Sherioux was burried 23 June. She was enjoyned to stand iij market daies in the town and iij Saboath daies in the church, in a white sheete, with a paper on her back and bosom showing her sinne, namely for unnatural incest with her own father. Her father the like, and her husband for being bawde. She stood with them one Saturday and one Sunday, and died the nexte.'

SUTTON VALLENCE, KENT. ' 1717, Nov. 25. On which day Eliz. Stace did public penance for y[e] foul sin of adultery committed with Thos. Hutchins jun[r] in Sutton Vallence Church, as did Anne ·Hynds for y[e] foul sin of fornication committed with Tho. Daws. SA: PRAT, *Vicar.*'

UXBRIDGE, MIDDLESEX. ' 1728. N.B. on July 7 Unity Winch did penance at morning service for 26 May.'
The register records on 26 May the baptism of her illegitimate child.

EAST PECKHAM, KENT. '1637. This yeare was the *communion table rayled in* by the appointment of Dr. Ryves, Chancellor to the Archbp. of Canterbury, who commanded this uniformity to be general throughout the kingdom.'
This mandate was strictly enforced, for the churchwardens of All Saints Church, Northampton, were excommunicated on 12 Jan. 1637–8, for disobeying the Archbishop's monition.[2]

[1] *Collect. Top. and Gen.* vol. iii. p. 93.
[2] *Calendar of State Papers.* Domestic, 1637–8.

SCOTTER, CO. LINCOLN. '1667–8, Jan. 19. Mem. That on Septua-
gesima Sunday, one Francis Drury, an excommunicate person,
came into the church in time of divine service in y⁰ morning, and
being admonisht by me to begon, hee obstinately refused, whereupon y⁰ whole congregation departed, and after the same manner
in the afternoon the same day he came againe, and refusing againe
to goe out, the whole congregation againe went home, soe yᵗ little
or noe service p'formed yᵗ day. I prevented his further coming in
yᵗ manner as he threatened, by order from the justice, upon the
statute of Q. Eliz. concerning the molestation and disturbance of
public preachers.

   ' WM. CARRINGTON, *Rector. O tempora! O mores!'*

This vigorous exercise of discipline would be more edifying,
if the penalty of excommunication had been reserved for grave
offences, and if we did not read in the same register,

 ' 1667–8. Mathew Whalley of Scawthorp was excommunicated
March 24, p' non solvendo taxat' eccl'iæ.'

Dispensations from the statutory obligation of abstaining
from meat during Lent were duly recorded in the register.

NEWINGTON, SURREY.[1] '1619. I, James Fludd, D.D., & Parson
of the Church of St. Mary, Newington, do give licence to Mrs.
Anna Jones of Newington, the wyfe of Evan Jones, Gent., being
notoriously sick, to eat flesh this time of Lent during the time of
sickness only, according to law in that case provided; videl. in the
5th of Eliz. and 1 Jacob. c. 29, provided alwaies that during the
time of her sickness she eat no beef, veale, porke, mutton, or bacon.
In witness whereof we have hereunto set our hand and seal. Dated
8 March 1619.'

Such dispensations were, before the reign of Elizabeth,
granted by the Sovereign as the head of the Church, and in 5
Edward VI., Sir Philip Hoby[2] obtained a licence under the Privy
Seal for himself and all who dined with him at his table during
his natural life,

' to eat meat and dishes made of milk either in Lent or on any other
fast days freely and without punishment.'

The law was so stringent in its provisions and so rigidly
enforced during the Primacy of Archbishop Laud, that when
the plague was raging in Hull, in 1636, and the Mayor and
Aldermen of that town petitioned the Archbishop of York for a
general dispensation for the townsmen to eat meat during the
ensuing Lent, on the grounds that a fish diet was likely to
increase the plague, and that Hull was ill-supplied with fish;
the Archbishop made answer to their petition, that the law did
not allow him to grant any such general licence, and that, in

----

[1] Manning and Bray's *Hist. of Surrey,* vol. iii. p. 452.
[2] Rymer's *Fœdera,* vol. xv. p. 291.

the event of sickness, individuals must obtain leave to eat flesh from their respective ministers, under certificate from a physician in each case. The rule during Lent was so universally observed at this period, that if we may trust the evidence of Taylor, the 'Water Poet,' the trade of the butchers was at a standstill for six weeks before Easter.

> 'The cutthroat butchers, wanting throats to cut,
> At Lent's approach their bloody shambles shut;
> For forty days their tyranny doth cease,
> And men and beasts take truce, and live in peace.'

Puritanical tendencies, however, were fast gaining ground, and the Puritans took singular pleasure in setting both law and custom at defiance. Taylor says [1] :

'I have often noted, that if any superfluous feasting or gormandizing, paunch-cramming assembly do meet, it is so ordered that it must be either in Lent, upon a Friday, or a fasting day: for the meat doth not relish well, except it be sauced with disobedience and contempt of authority. And though they eat sprats on a Sunday, they care not, so that they may be full gorged with flesh on the Friday night.

> '"Then all the zealous puritans will feast
> In detestation of the Romish beast." '

The legal obligation of abstaining from meat was continued from time to time by various statutes, the last of which (16 Charles I., chap. i.) declared such enactments to be

'Revived and continued until some other Act of Parliament be made touching the continuance or discontinuance thereof.'

No such other act was ever passed, and when, in 1687, abstinence from meat during Lent was enjoined by the King's proclamation, it was advertised in the *London Gazette*[2] that an office was opened in St. Paul's Churchyard where licences to eat flesh in any part of England could be obtained on condition of giving alms to the poor. Since the Revolution of 1688, no attempt has ever been made to put these statutes in force, but they remained a dead letter in the Statute book until 1863, when they were repealed in a mass by the Statute Law Revision Act.

It would seem that itinerant showmen of the Barnum type were not unknown in England three centuries ago.

St. Nicholas, Durham.[3] '1568. Mem'd'm, that a certaine Italian brought into the cittie of Durham, the 11th day of June, in the year above sayd, a very greate strange and monstrous serpent,

---

[1] *JackaLent*, by Taylor.
[2] *London Gazette*, Sept. 22, 1687.
[3] Surtees' *Hist. of Co. Durham.*

in length sixteene feate, in quantitie and dimentions greater than a
greate horse, which was taken and killed by speciall policie, Œthiopia
within the Turkas dominions. But before it was killed, it had
devoured (as it is credibly thought) more than 1,000 persons, and
destroyed a whole countrey.'

The solemn renunciation of a boy by his parents to his
master and adopted father was thought worthy of insertion in
the register of the parish of St. Olave's, in the Old Jewry, and is
attested by the vicar.

St. Olave's, Jewry, London. '1591, May 2. Mem. That I
William Corsse and Mary Corsse do here, in the parish of St. Olave,
this present day, in the presence of us, whose names are here under-
written, willingly, freely, and voluntarily, give our son, Pasfeld
Corsse, unto John Callcock, of London, Grocer, as freely as it pleased
Almighty God to give him unto us, the 14th day of Feb. 1586,
being Ash Wednesday, he being five years old and better, and
having been with yᵉ said John Callcock now one year. And we
promise further not to have to do with our said son Pasfeld during
the life of the said John Callcock, otherwise than to be humble
petitioners unto Almighty God for the health of our said dear son,
and the prosperity of John Callcock his said master. And in
witness of the truth unto these premises we have put our hands the
day and year above said, viz.

' WILLIAM CORSSE,   ' MARY CORSSE,
' WILLIAM DAVIES, *Vicar*,   ' NYCHˢ. COKSON.'
' WILLIAM PERIE,

Briefs, or royal letters patent of recommendation, authorising collections for charitable purposes, were publicly read in
parish churches, when the amount collected and the object of
the collection were entered in the parish register. When the
Civil War broke out, the House of Commons took precautions
against the royal prerogative being exercised in issuing briefs
to raise money for the supply of the King's wants, or for the
relief of sufferers in the royal cause; and on Jan. 31, 1643,
Henry Martin, afterwards known as the regicide, brought in
'an order for inhibiting any collections upon any brief under
the Great Seal.'[1] A further order was made on Jan. 10, 1648,[1]
that no collections should be made on briefs, except such as
were issued under the Great Seal, under direction of both Houses
of Parliament, and under this order a collection was authorised
on May 31, 1653, on occasion of a great fire at Marlborough.
After the Restoration, briefs became an abuse, and Pepys has
the following note in his *Diary*:

'1661, June 30, Sunday. To Church, where we observe the

---

[1] *Journals of the House of Commons.*

trade of briefs is come now up to so constant a course every Sunday, that we resolve to give no more to them.'

This note will account for the ludicrously small amount of many of these collections.

STOCK HARWARD, ESSEX.[1] '1661, Dec. 8. Collected on a Brief concerning 100 Protestant Churches in the Dukedom of Lithuania, 3 shillings and 3 pence.'

CHEADLE, CHESHIRE. '1661. Collected on the same Brief, 4 shillings.'

SPRINGTHORPE, CO. LINCOLN. '1690, July 26. Collected for Teignmouth, for loss by the French landing firing and plundering the said town, 2s. 10d.'

STOCK HARWARD.[1] '1707, May 4. Towcester Brief, lost by fire, £1057 ; collected 9½d.'

'1708, April 25. Brief for Lisburn, in Ireland ; lost by fire, £31,770 ; collected, sevenpence ! '

Appeals for the redemption of Englishmen out of slavery were better responded to.

SCRAPLOFT, CO. LEICESTER. '1679, July 28. Collected, to redeem Thomas, son of Mr. Owsley, Rector of Glooston, taken by the Algerines, £1. 11s. 3d. ! '

WEEDON BECK, NORTHAMPTONSHIRE. '1680, Aug. 9. Collected for y* redemption of Christians (taken by y* Turkish Pyrates) out of Turkish slavery, £1. 8s. 0d.'

The danger of being sold into captivity by Mediterranean pirates was so well appreciated at the end of the seventeenth century, that there were insurance offices [2] in London and other capitals, where an insurance could be effected to provide the ransom exacted by the pirates.

Briefs are mentioned in the Rubric of the Prayer Book of 1662, and so long as there was no means of insuring against losses by fire and flood, something of the kind was wanted to relieve individual sufferers and spread the loss over a larger area. But briefs were a clumsy expedient, and it was soon found that the success of the collection depended less on the merits of the cause than on the skill with which the machinery was worked. This led to a bad system of farming briefs by professional undertakers, who contrived to put into their own pockets the lion's share of the proceeds. The abuses of this system engaged the attention of Parliament [3] in 1704, and an Act was passed in the next year ' for the better collecting charity

---

[1] *Journal of Archæol. Institute*, vol. xxxvii. p. 410.
[2] *Insurance Cyclopædia*, by C. Walford. See *Captivity*.
[3] *King's Briefs*, by C. Walford, 1882, contains a full account of these proceedings, and an exhaustive history of Briefs.

money on Briefs, preventing abuses in relation thereto.'[1] By
this Act the Lord Chancellor was empowered to grant briefs for
what he considered deserving objects, and a machinery was
created for dealing with the proceeds. There were offices' in
existence at this period to insure houses against fire, although
their operations, until 1710, did not extend beyond the bills of
mortality. It might, therefore, be expected, that under the
reformed system a brief would be withheld, when the loss was
occasioned by the wilful neglect of the sufferer to insure. Bowyer
the printer,[2] however, obtained a brief from Lord Chancellor
Cowper in 1713, under which £1,514. 13s. 4d. was collected
towards making good his losses by the fire, which consumed his
premises and stock in trade on Jan. 12, 1712.

The statutory fees to patent officers and the charges of the
King's Printers made briefs an inconvenient and expensive
mode of raising money for charitable purposes ; insomuch that
the charges of collecting £614. 12s. 9d. for repairing a church in
Westmorland amounted to £330. 16s. 6d., leaving only £283.
16s. 3d. for the charity.[3] Statutory briefs accordingly fell into
disrepute, and were abolished by Act of Parliament in 1828,[4]
but the royal prerogative was not affected by the statute, and
Queen's letters have been granted on several occasions during
the present reign in aid of the Society for the Propagation of the
Gospel, and other favoured charities.

CHAPEL ROYAL, WHITEHALL. '1676, Nov. 19. Monsieur Martin
Breton, a priest and preacher at St. Paul's Church at Paris, made
his recantacŏn in the Chappell after Evening Prayer, imediately
before the Grace of o͏ʳ L͏ᵈ Jesus X͏ᵗ &c. He declared his unfeigned
sorrow ·y͏ᵗ he had bin so long detained in the Ch. of Rome, and
promis'd as long as his life should last he would bee a true Son of
the Church of England. In testimony whereof he gave it under
his hand openly, to the Ld. Bp. of London, then Dean of the
Chappell.'
It would scarcely have been expected that a convert from
Popery would obtain preferment in the reign of James II., but
Martin Breton was presented, in May 1687, by the Governors of
St. Bartholomew's Hospital, to the vicarages of Great and Little
Wakering, Essex, and he continued to hold both livings in
1700.[5]

HAMBLEDON, BUCKS. '1685, May 17. Mary Wallington had a
certificate to goe before the King for a disease called the King's
Evil.'

[1] 4 Anne, c. 14.
[2] Nichols's *Literary Anecdotes*, vol. i. p. 57.
[3] Burns's *Ecclesiastical Law*, tit. *Briefs*.
[4] 9 Geo. IV. c. 28.
[5] Newcourt's *Repertorium*, vol. ii. p. 621.

No one was allowed to enter the King's presence for the purpose of being touched for the Evil, without a certificate from the minister of the parish from which he came, that he had never been touched before; and every minister was required by a proclamation of Charles II., dated Jan. 9, 1683, to keep a register of the certificates which he granted. This regulation was found necessary to keep down the numbers, for no less than 92,107 persons came to be touched between 1661 and 1682, and every one them had a gold coin, with a hole in it, given to him, which was suspended from the neck by a ribbon. The expense and superstition of this practice were equally distasteful to William III., and he was the first King of England who positively refused to touch patients. His refusal, however, was interpreted as a confession that he was no rightful King; and Queen Anne's ministers thought it politic to revive an ancient observance, which was calculated to confirm the lower orders in their loyalty to the sovereign. Accordingly, it was officially announced in the Gazette of March 12, 1712, that Her Majesty would touch and heal persons afflicted with the Evil at certain appointed times, and it was on this occasion that Johnson was touched, by the advice of Sir John Floyer, the physician at Lichfield. Barrington also mentions an old man, who swore in Court that when he was a child he was touched for the Evil, and was cured by Queen Anne at Oxford. Barrington asked him if he was really cured, when he answered that, he doubted in his own mind whether he ever had the Evil, but his ' parents were poor, and had no objection to the bit of gold.'[1]

The Royal prerogative was jealously guarded, and James Philip Gandre, a French knight of the order of St. Lazare, was was sent to prison by Lord Chief Justice Richardson on June 7, 1632,

' For committing a contempt worthy of punishment, in taking upon himself to cure the King's Evil.'

BRENTFORD, MIDDLESEX. '1698, Feb. 26. Alice and Elizabeth Pickering, wandering children, were whipped according to law, and sent with a pass to Shrewsbury, the place where they were born.' Under the vagrant laws, which remained in force until 1744, any persons found begging,

' Were, by the appointment of the head-borough or tithing man, assisted by the advice of the minister of the parish, to be openly whipped till they were bloody, and then sent from parish to parish until they came to the parish in which they were born.'

TURNWORTH, DORSET. '1747. On Ascension Day, after morning prayer at Turnworth Church, was made a publick Perambulation

---

[1] *Barrington on Ancient Statutes*, p. 107.

of yᵉ bounds of yᵉ parish of Turnworth, by one Richd. Cobbe, vicar, Wm. Northover, churchwarden, Henry Sillers and Richard Mullen, overseers, and others, with 4 boys; beginning at the Church Hatch and cutting a great T on the most principal parts of the bounds. Whipping yᵉ boys by way of remembrance, and stopping their cry with some half-pence; we returned to church again, which Perambulation and Possessioning had not been made for 20 years last past.'[1]

We must now in candour expose some of the defects of the old system of trusting entirely to the discretion of the clergyman to keep the registers in his own fashion. That the registers were carelessly and negligently kept in many parishes was a scandal which engaged the attention of the Lower House of Convocation in the reign of Queen Anne. A Committee was appointed in the winter of 1702–3 to draw up a list of ecclesiastical offences, which notoriously required remedy, and the charge of irregularity in the parish registers was prominent in the list of *gravamina.* It must be confessed, however, that in some of the following extracts the clergyman must be charged with something worse than mere carelessness.

TUNSTALL, KENT. '1557. Mary Pottman nat. and bapt. 15 Apr. Mary Pottman nat. and bapt. 29th June. Mary Pottman sep. 22 Aug. From henceforward I omit the Pottmans.'

PETERBOROUGH. '1604. Here it seemeth that the Byll of the names of such as were baptized, marryed, or buryed in the month of April, 1604, was utterly lost, and never could be found to be sette down afterwards in the church register. Ita testor, Edward Wager, vicar.'

MEOPHAM, KENT. 'In the daies of Mr. James Day, vicar of Mepham for fyve yers space, none were registered.'

STOKE NEWINGTON. '1617 to 1619, *a long vacation.*'

BITTESWELL, CO. LEIC. 1638. 'Mary Snelson is stark naught, stinking naught. Blot not this.'

ST. PETER'S, DORCHESTER. '1645. In twelve months there died 52 persons, whose names are not inserted, the old clark being dead who had the notes.'

MELTON MOWBRAY. 1670. 'Here is a bill of Burton Lazars the people, which was buried and which was and maried (*sic*), above 10 years old, for because the clarke was dead and therefore they was not set down according as they was, but they all set down sure enough one amon ganother here in this place.'

ST. EWE, CORNWALL. '1677. The parishioners refusing to allow 5*s*. per annum for keeping a register, there was none kept for the years 1675-6-7, only these two baptisms were put down by me Joseph May, clerk.'

SEA SALTER, KENT. '1734. John Ponney, of Canterbury, huntsman to that ancient Corporation of Cuckolds, and Elizabeth Johnson,

[1] Hutchins's *Hist. of Dorset.*

daughter of the Devil's Vicegerent, commonly called a Bailiff, were trammell'd at the Cathedral of Sea Salter, April 26.'

'1734, June 6, John Housden, Widower, a gape-mouthed lazy fellow, and Hannah Matthews, hot-a-pon't, an old toothless wriggling hag, both of Faversham, were trammell'd by licence at the Cathedral, Sea Salter, a Caspian bowl of well-acidulated Glimigrim.'

1734, Oct. 29. 'Old Tom Taylor, the great smoker of Whitstable, and a deaf old woman called Elizabeth Church, were married at Sea Salter with two rings. Si quis ex successoribus nostris hoc forte legat, rideat si velit.'

SHILLINGSTONE, DORSET. '1742, Jan. 1. David Pitman and Mary Haskell, a rogue and a whore, married.'

FELTHAM, MIDDX. '   of this parish, and   of   parish, were married in this   by   this 1st day of Decr 1770 by me

This marre was solemnised between us { Elizabeth × West '

RAMSDEN BELLHOUSE, ESSEX. '1772, Aug. 24. Samuel Douset (Ebrius, iracundus, inops, miserandus abivit) sepultus.'

HINDRINGHAM, NORFOLK. '1782. Dec. 9, Register of baptisms and burials from 1749, and of marriages from 1747, neglected by Mr. Hemington, curate, to this day.'

Some of these extracts simply denote extreme and exceptional negligence, but others point to a mischievous practice which has never been positively prohibited by law, and which has been a constant source of error and deficiency. I refer to the practice of omitting to make the entries at the time, and of leaving it to the clerk to keep rough notes, which were at uncertain intervals transcribed into the Register-books. The clerk's notes often made sad havoc with the names, which he spelled on the rudest principle of the phonetic system. The following entries are all intended to denote the name and family of William Methold,[1] the founder of the Methold Almshouses at Kensington, which remained unaltered with their quaint gables, as they were built in the time of the Commonwealth, until they were pulled down in 1865 by the Metropolitan Railway Company under their statutory powers.

KENSINGTON. '1648, April 16. Edward Mathowld, bur.'

'1648, July 27, Thos., son of Mr. Willm Methell, Esq., bapt.'

'1652, March 10. Mr. William Meathell, bur.'

'1675, Mch. 7, Susanna dau. of Mr. Willm Methold, bur.'

'1681, Mch. 2, William son of Thos. Methwold, gent., bapt.'

---

[1] William Methold, buried 10 March 1652-3, was the first Englishman who visited the diamond mines of Golconda, and the narrative of his Indian travels was printed in 1626 in the fifth volume of Purchas's *Pilgrims*. On his return from Surat in 1635, he purchased from the executors of Sir William Blake, Hale House, Kensington, with a park of 66 acres within the manor of Earl's Court, which is now known as the Harrington estate. This mansion, afterwards known as Cromwell House, remained standing until 1850, when it was pulled down to form a site for the Great Exhibition.

KIRKBY MOORSIDE, YORKSHIRE. ' 1687. Georges vilaus Lord dooke of bookingham, bur. 17 April.'

This rude illspelt entry of his burial supplies the last finishing touch to Pope's well-known description of the neglected death-bed of the ' Great Villiers.'

In another case, vouched by Sir Thomas Phillipps,[1] a gentleman named *Anchetil* Grey found on examining the register of his baptism that he had been entered as *Miss Ann Kettle Grey*.

False spelling and the consequent difficulty of identifying names were not the only evils, which resulted from trusting to the clerk's notes. The notes were often lost or mislaid before they were copied, and where the clerk kept a day-book, it constantly happened that the Parish Register was not a full and accurate transcript. This is so well known to historical students, that they habitually make search among the church records for the original memoranda, when they examine the registers for a literary purpose. I give two instances from St. Saviour's, Southwark,[2] of the omission from the register-books of interesting information, positively identifying the deceased, which is given in the original notes. The register says :

' 1608. Laurence Fletcher, a man, bur. in the church, 12 Sept.'
' 1625. Mr. John Fletcher, a man, bur. in the church, 29 Aug.'

The original entries of these burials, in the unbound sheets still preserved in the vestry, run thus :

' 1608. Laurence Fletcher, a *player*, the *king's servant*, bur. in the church 12 Sept., with an afternoon's knell of the great bell.'
' 1625. John Fletcher, a *poet*, bur. in the church, Aug. 29.'

Such variations have in legal proceedings proved of most serious consequence. ' In May *v.* May,[3] the day-book was produced to prove that the plaintiff was on his baptism registered as " base-born," although such addition was omitted in the Register ; and although it was proved by the clerk that the Register was made up every three months from this very day-book, the Court decided that there could not be two registers in one parish, and therefore that the false entry which implied the plaintiff's legitimacy must prevail.' In another case,[4] it was decided that the clerk's notes were mere private entries and not admissible in evidence, and that a baptism dated Feb. 6, 1776, but not copied into the Register until June 1777, could not be received, because the entry had been made solely

---

[1] Evidence of Sir Thos. Phillipps, June 25, 1833.
[2] Collier's *Memoirs of Actors*, 1846, pp. x–xii.
[3] May *v.* May. 2 Strange, p. 272.
[4] Doe dem. Warren *v.* Bray. 8 Barnewall, p. 813.

on the information of the clerk. Lord Eldon, in a formal judgment,[1] declared that 'not one register in a hundred had been kept according to the canon.' And in the Chandos Peerage Case grave doubts were suggested in the House of Lords by Lord Rosslyn, whether all Parish Registers should not be rejected in evidence, on the ground that *none of them* had been kept according to law. It should be borne in mind, that although the injunction of 1538 and the Canon of 1603 had ordered that the Register-book be made up on Sundays, this was not intended to authorise delay in registration, but rather to recognise the growing custom of solemnising baptisms, &c., on Sundays only. This innovation was displeasing to the followers of the old religion, for the sixth of the fifteen Articles of Complaint alleged by the Rebels of Devon[2] in 1549 was,

'we will that our curates shall minister the sacrament of baptism at all times, as well in the weekday as on the holyday.'

It might have been expected that Rose's Act would have remedied this acknowledged evil by a peremptory enactment; but an interval of seven days is still allowed to the clergyman to make the entries, and there is no penalty attached in cases when the prescribed period is exceeded. The consequence has been, that in many parishes[3] the law is openly and habitually disregarded, and that it is still the practice to make up the register from a rough book kept by the clerk at intervals of a month and upwards.

Another point which Rose's Act left unsettled was the question of fees, for it simply directed 'that all due, legal, and accustomed fees' for making entries in the register and giving certified copies 'should be paid as heretofore,' whilst nothing is said about any fee for searching the registers. It had always been held that the clergy were entitled to some fees for producing their registers for examination, and for giving certified extracts; but there was no uniform fee for such services, and the amount, which varied in different parishes, was usually fixed by a table of fees suspended in the vestry, which was assumed to have been approved at some time or other by the Bishop or his archdeacon. Such fees in former times were considered the perquisite of the Curate, but when the Rector was a married man, it was a common complaint that his wife

---

[1] Walker *v.* Wingfield. 18 Vesey, p. 443.

[2] *Cranmer's Works.* Parker Society Edition, vol. i. p. 175.

[3] Mr. Parr, clerk of St. Saviour's, Southwark, stated to the Committee of 1833 that he made all the entries in a rough book, which was copied into the register at 'various periods of *three or four or five months.*' The parish clerk of St. Matthew's, Bethnal Green, deposed that his rough notes of marriages and burials were posted about once a month.

insisted on sharing them. According to a curious tract printed in 1641, and entitled, ' *The Curates' Conference; or a Discourse betwixt two Scholars, both of them relating their Hard Condition and consulting which way to mend it,*'

' The Rector's wife takes out of the Curate's wages half of every funeral sermon, and out of all burials, churchings, weddings, christenings, &c., she hath half duties to buy lace, pins, gloves, fans, blackbags, satin petticoats, &c.'

Before the Civil Registration Act of 1836 it was assumed to be law, that the public had no right to search the registers at all, except by the favour of the clergyman and churchwardens. Chief Justice Tenterden judicially declared :[1]

' I know of no rule of law which requires the parish officers to show the books, in order to gratify the curiosity of a private individual.'

The Act of 1836 fixes a uniform scale of fees both for searches and certificates, but the case of extracts not certified by the minister is not provided for. It is enacted that

' every Rector, Vicar, or Curate, who has the keeping of any register book of births, deaths, or marriages, shall at all reasonable times allow searches to be made of any register book in his keeping, on payment of one shilling for a search of one year, and sixpence for every additional year, and of two shillings and sixpence for every entry certified under his hand as a true copy of the register.'

It was contended, however, by some of the clergy, that this enactment was limited to births and deaths, and that it did not extend to baptisms and burials ; and, moreover, that persons searching the register had no right to take extracts unless they were certified by the minister, which involved an additional fee of two-and-sixpence for each extract. This claim was practically prohibitory to a general search for literary purposes, and an action was brought in the Court of Exchequer to test the legality of so heavy a tax on historical research. The Court decided[2] in Easter term, 1853, that the fees for searching registers of baptisms and burials between 1827 and 1830 were regulated by the Act of 1836 ; that a person paying for a search was entitled to make whatever extracts he pleased during the period for which he had paid the search fee ; and that no further payment could be demanded for certificates, unless the person searching required the extract to be certified by the minister. In the absence of any statutory fee for extracts, the Judges seem to have considered that every extract should be paid for as a separate search, for in this case 25 extracts were taken during a

---

[1] Rex *v.* Smallpiece, 2 Chitty's *Reports*, p. 288.
[2] Steele *v.* Williams. Exchequer *Reports*, viii., p. 825.

period extending over four years, and the fee allowed was thirteen shillings.

The Act of 1812 has never been repealed, and the registers of baptism and burial are still governed by its provisions, but they have lost much of their former importance since 1837, when the new system of civil registration came into operation. How and why this change was brought about remains to be told.

It seems almost superfluous in the present day to insist upon the advantages of an accurate system of registration. In all the common concerns of life, in the acts of buying selling and marrying, in questions of pedigree inheritance and legitimacy, our rights and interests are so frequently dependent upon the fulness and correctness of the public registers, that they seem almost a necessary element of our complex civilisation. Nor are they less useful to the community than to individuals; for they form the basis of political arithmetic, and supply the data for determining with precision the progress and condition of the people.

A system, which ran counter to the feelings and interests of a numerous class, could never permanently satisfy the conditions of national registration, and Dissenters of all denominations were practically excluded from parish registers by their unwillingness to be baptized, married, and buried by the parochial clergy.

Parish registers were instituted at a period when all Englishmen professed the same religion; and so long as every infant was baptized on the day of its birth, and the dead were all buried with the same ritual, births and deaths were sufficiently recorded in the parish registers of baptisms and burials, and no one was aggrieved by registration being left to the clergy. But when religious uniformity ceased to be the law of the land, and Dissenters became a recognised and tolerated body with registers of their own, it was felt as a grievance that the registers of Dissenting chapels were not accepted as evidence in courts of justice. This grievance was resented by numbers increasing every year, and was aggravated as time went on by complaints of a breach of faith. The Stamp Act[1] was extended in 1785 to non-parochial registers at the petition of the Dissenters, on the understanding that taxation would impress on them a public character, and that the Government stamp would make them admissible as legal evidence; but, although the tax was paid for ten years, the expected equivalent was withheld. Dissenters of all denominations had since 1740 regis-

---

[1] 25 Geo. III. cap. 75.

tered the births of their children in a Library in Red Cross Street, Cripplegate, which was known by the name of the founder, Dr. Daniel Williams. A certificate on parchment, signed by the parents and friends in duplicate, was filed at the Library, and the particulars were entered in a book in a tabular form. This register was kept with great care, and was authenticated in 1840 by Act[1] of Parliament, but in the meanwhile the Master of the Rolls refused to accept it as evidence that a ward had attained his majority.[2] In like manner, the Judge of the Prerogative Court judicially allowed in 1811 the objection taken to the register of a Dissenting chapel, that it was not a public document in official custody.[3] A statutory exception was made in 1817 in the case of subscribers to a new Government[4] Loan, many of whom were Dissenters. The Commissioners for the Reduction of the National Debt were expressly authorised by the terms of the Act to accept the certificate of burial recorded in a Dissenting chapel as evidence of the death of a nominee; but in all other cases non-parochial registers were ignored until the Reform Act of 1832 transferred the balance of political power. In the meanwhile, the abolition of the Test and Corporation Act in 1828 changed the legal *status* of the Dissenters, and raised them from being a mere tolerated body to an equal participation in civil and political rights; but the unreformed Parliament was slow to meddle with the privileges of the clergy, and it was not without opposition that a clause was inserted in the Census Act of 1830, which obliged the minister and churchwardens of every parish to make a return of all the registers in their possession of earlier date than 1813, when Rose's Act came into operation.

Registration was one of the first questions which engaged attention in the Reformed Parliament, and in the Session of 1833 a Select Committee was appointed for the two-fold purpose of inquiring into the actual state of parish registers, and of devising an improved scheme of general registration. At the same time the Return made in pursuance of the Act of 1830 was ordered to be printed for the guidance of the Committee, which had special instructions to inquire into the working of the Act of 1812. Their labours were embodied in an elaborate and exhaustive Report, in which the deplorable condition of the registers and the negligence of their legal custodians were exposed by antiquaries and other experts, whilst the anomalies

[1] 3 & 4 Vict. cap. 92.
[2] *Ex parte* Taylor, 1 Jacob and Walker, 483.
[3] Newham *v.* Raithby, Trinity Term, 1811.
[4] 57 Geo. III. cap. 26.

of the English system were contrasted with the provisions of the *Code Napoléon*, and with the forms used in other countries where civil registration prevails. The evidence collected by the Committee supplied conclusive proof that the old system had completely broken down under the strain of modern requirements, and that even if parish registers had been better kept and preserved than they had been, a new scheme based on a different principle was imperatively called for.

It was a radical defect in parish registers that they were based on the transparent fiction, that the State Church was co-extensive with the nation, and that the whole population were baptized and buried by the parochial clergy. It is manifest that no scheme could be effective which ignored the Dissenters, and they refused to accept a system which left the exclusive control in the hands of the clergy. Registration is in itself a purely civil act, which has properly no connexion whatever with religion. The duty of keeping registers was imposed on the clergy by the Civil Power under different conditions of society from those which now prevail; and the ecclesiastical character, which was impressed on registers in an age of religious uniformity, became an element of discord and disturbance in a generation distracted by a myriad of contending sects. The connexion of registers with the Church was of political origin, and there was no good reason for maintaining it when it ceased to be politically expedient. The principles of civil and religious equality were violated by the monopoly of the clergy, and the problem of reconciling the conflicting claims of conscience and liberty could only be solved by divesting registration of its religious character.

Public opinion insisted that in an age of baptismal controversies, register office marriages, and unconsecrated cemeteries, individuals should be left to baptize marry and bury in the fashion which their several consciences dictated and their religion prescribed, and that the action of the Government should be limited to the registration of births deaths and marriages, which are overt acts affecting society. These conditions could only be satisfied by the enactment of a general system of civil registration ; and after a severe political struggle, an Act[1] was passed in 1836, by which the registers of baptisms and burials were left undisturbed to the care of the parochial clergy, whilst the State assumed, for the first time, the duty of registering in one public office the births, marriages, and deaths of the whole population, irrespectively of their religious belief.

This enactment, however, would not have satisfied the Dis-

---

[1] 6 & 7 William IV. c. 86, amended by 1 Vict. c. 22.

senters unless some provision had been made to authenticate existing non-parochial registers; and it was an element of difficulty that many of them had been badly kept and were confessedly invalidated by irregularity. To meet this difficulty a Royal Commission was issued, by which skilled and impartial Commissioners were empowered to inquire into the state, custody, and authenticity of existing non-parochial registers, and to report what measures could be beneficially adopted for collecting, arranging, and depositing the same, and for giving them full force and effect as evidence in courts of justice. The Commissioners brought in their report on June 18, 1838, recommending that about 3,000 volumes which they had collected and authenticated should be deposited with the Registrar-General and should be made receivable in evidence, subject to certain conditions and restrictions. Their recommendations were carried into effect by Act of Parliament on August 10, 1840.[1] This experiment was so successful, that, by the recommendation of another Royal Commission which was appointed on January 1, 1857, the provisions of the Act of 1840 were extended in 1858 to 265 other registers, which had been collected since 1838;[2] so that the Nonconformists have no longer any reasonable ground of complaint.

The parish register Acts had never extended to Scotland or Ireland, and the Government of 1836 was too indifferent to legislation which promised no party advantages, and too apprehensive of exciting religious prejudice north of the Tweed, to propose that this Act should extend to Scotland, although the defective state of the Scottish registers had more than once been the subject of official censure,[3] and had been severely commented upon by writers[4] of acknowledged ability. The Provincial Council of the Scottish clergy had instituted registers of baptisms and marriages so far back as 1551, with a declaration that these records should be preserved among 'the most precious treasures of the Church;' and this ordinance had been confirmed and extended to burials by the Privy Council of Scotland in 1616. But these decrees had been so imperfectly observed, that out of 850 parishes which made

---

[1] 3 & 4 Vict. cap. 92. Amongst the registers authenticated by this Act were those of the French and other Protestant refugees, the Wesleyan and Calvinistic Methodists. Moravians, Lady Huntingdon's Connexion, Swedenborgians, the Society of Friends, and the Registries of Redcross Street, Dr. Williams' Library, Bunhill Fields and Paternoster Row.

[2] 21 Vict. cap. 25. This Act includes the registers of the Greenwich, Chelsea, and Foundling Hospitals.

[3] Report of the Deputy Clerk Register of Scotland to the Commissioners of Public Records in 1810.

[4] Sir John Sinclair's *Statistical Account of Scotland.*

returns to Government in the Population Abstract of 1801, only 99 were in possession of regular registers. The Scotch are proverbially jealous of parliamentary interference with their ecclesiastical ordinances. But the shrewdness of the national character inclined them to sacrifice a prejudice, which was incompatible with their interests; and accordingly the royal assent was given on August 7, 1854, to an Act [1] establishing a civil registration for Scotland, as similar in its leading features to the English Act of 1836 as the different customs of the two countries would allow.

But the wants of Ireland were less carefully provided for; although the only Irish registers were those of the Established Church, which are a dead letter for five-sixths of the population; and the Imperial Parliament contented itself with enacting in 1844 a civil registration [2] for Protestant marriages.

It is a positive fact that until January 1, 1864, the births and deaths of the entire population of Ireland, and the marriages of the Catholic majority, were suffered to remain wholly unregistered. This anomaly had not continued from any want of notice to those who were able to remove it and were interested in its removal. Year after year, the House of Lords had been besieged with complaints that the claimants of peerages were unable to substantiate an Irish pedigree, from the absence of registers; in the criminal courts, juries had been disabled from convicting for bigamy by the difficulty of proving the prior marriage; and in the civil courts, the kindred of emigrants dying intestate in America had, from the want of legal evidence, been constantly defrauded of their natural inheritance. Twelve reports of the Irish Registrar-General had in vain urged upon successive Parliaments the duty of supplying this national want; and when the Government at last proposed a partial remedy, it was as much due to the scandal of the Yelverton case as to an enlarged consideration of the public welfare.

In February 1863 the Government brought in a Bill to establish civil registration in Ireland; but this measure was restricted to births and deaths, and made no provision whatever for Catholic marriages. It may be alleged that this omission was forced upon the authors of the Bill by the anomalies of the Irish marriage laws, and the jealousy of Catholics to allow parliamentary interference with the administration of a sacrament. But the hardships attending mixed marriages affect comparatively few, whilst the absence of registers is a serious evil to the whole community. Civil registration prevails

[1] 17 & 18 Vict. c. 80.
[2] 7 & 8 Vict. c. 81, amended by 26 Vict. c. 27.

in many Catholic countries on the Continent, and has been accepted by the Catholics of England and Scotland; and there seems no good reason why Catholics should be unwilling on one side of the Channel to conform to regulations which are cheerfully complied with on the other. An attempt, however, was made by the leading Catholics in Parliament, to distinguish the case of marriages from that of births and deaths; and the Government adopted the distinction. But marriage is not only a sacrament but a civil contract, involving social and political obligations properly cognisable by the State; and the State has therefore the same right to insist upon its registration as upon that of any other contract. The validity of a marriage *in foro conscientiæ* must always be distinct from the question of its registration; the registry-book is obviously the record of an act, and not the act itself; and even if, in a few isolated cases, another chapter be thereby added to the conflict of laws, the balance of advantages will be found greatly in favour of civil registration.

The Bill passed without amendment,[1] but its omissions were so generally condemned by public opinion, that the new system was before the end of the Session extended by a separate Act to Catholic marriages. This Act[2] left untouched the vexed question of the marriage laws, and therefore recognised the precise distinction which I have attempted to draw between the validity of a marriage and its registration. Both Acts have been in force since January 1, 1864.

The Irish Registration Laws were framed upon the plan of the Scottish Act of 1854; but they wholly omit one of its most important features, by failing to provide for the preservation and custody of existing registers. The Scottish Act requires all parochial registers minutes and documents of every description before 1824, relating to births deaths and marriages, to be deposited with the Registrar-General; and no reason can be alleged for exempting Ireland from similar provisions. The Irish parish registers have been quite as badly kept and preserved as the Scottish, and notoriously stand in equal need of protection against accident and negligence. Their existence was ignored by the Act for disestablishing[3] the Church in Ireland, and therefore, since January 1, 1871, they have been wholly divested of their official and national character. There are also other Irish registers in existence, which, under certain conditions and restrictions, could usefully be made available as evidence. The Protestant Dissenters have their own records;

---

[1] 26 Vict. c. 11.   [2] 26 & 27 Vict. c. 90.   [3] 32 & 33 Vict. c. 42.

and we know[1] that of late years the Catholic Bishops have required their parish priests to keep regular registers in the form prescribed by the Council of Trent. Now, it is obviously of the highest importance to the public that all these registers should be collected, kept in safe custody, and made readily accessible, and that so many of them as can be authenticated by competent authority should be declared by Act of Parliament admissible as evidence in courts of justice. It is to be hoped, therefore, that the provisions of the Scottish Registration Act will be extended to Ireland, and that the registers of the Irish Catholics and Protestant Dissenters will be placed on the same footing as the English non-parochial registers, by the appointment of a Royal Commission to collect and authenticate them. There are two precedents for such a course; and if there be any Protestants who would grudge to the Catholics of Ireland this act of justice, we would remind them of the language of the Catholic king Lewis XVI.:

'We confess that in allowing the Protestant [minority of France] the permission to have their births, marriages, and deaths legally verified, so that they may reap the same civil advantages therefrom as our other subjects, we allow no more than what the law of nature does not suffer us to refuse.'

The present system of civil registration, which collects in one central office the births and deaths of the whole population of England in books alphabetically indexed, has practically superseded the modern registers of baptism and burial. But the parish registers previous to 1837 are every year becoming of greater value as national records. They are not only indispensable to the local historian, and invaluable to the biographer, but they have for a long time been the only public documents in existence for determining questions of inheritance; for the Heralds' visitations were confined to the gentry, and were discontinued in the seventeenth century. No one, therefore, will now dispute the importance of preserving with the utmost care all those registers, which time accident and negligence have spared to us.

But this unfortunately was not the feeling which prevailed in former times, when public opinion was worse than indifferent to their safety. In the last century the parish register was generally left at the mercy of the parish clerk, who was always illiterate and often corrupt, so that there was practically no safeguard whatever against fraud, if any unscrupulous person cared to tamper with the register. The proceedings in the case of the notorious Duchess of Kingston supply a striking

---

[1] Evidence of Rev. P. O'Regan before the Committee of the House of Commons, June 26, 1861.

example in point. When that lady imagined that it would answer her purpose to destroy the evidence of her secret marriage with Captain Hervey, she found no difficulty in obtaining access to the register of the church in which she was married, and in tearing out the leaf in which the marriage was recorded. At a later period, when Hervey succeeded to the Earldom of Bristol, and it suited her purpose to uphold the marriage, she found it equally easy to replace the leaf in the register by a bribe to the parish clerk. But apart from fraud, parish registers were in the last century exposed to every form of destruction which ignorance and carelessness could devise.[1] They were cut up for patterns by tailors and lacemakers, mutilated by collectors of autographs, and sold for waste paper, almost without remonstrance, except from a few indignant antiquaries. The parchment books suffered more than the paper ones, from the greater number of uses to which the materials could be turned. In one parish in Sussex[2] they were cut up by the clergyman into slips, which he used as labels for addressing baskets of game; and when Mr. Bell inquired for the early registers at Christchurch, in Hampshire, for the purpose of producing them in the House of Lords as evidence in the Huntingdon peerage case, he found that they had been converted into kettle-holders by the wife of a former curate.[3] It may safely be affirmed that the negligence of the eighteenth century was more destructive than the civil wars of the seventeenth. Mr. Baker, the historian of Northamptonshire,[4] found that out of the nine registers commencing in 1538, which were examined by Mr. Bridges in 1718 for his History of the County, only four survived in 1826; and that out of seventy parish registers which were searched by Bridges, sixteen had perished in the interval.

The growing taste for antiquarian studies, and an increased sense of responsibility amongst the clergy, has arrested the course of destruction, and with some allowance for losses by fire and damp the existing registers are accurately described in the Parish Register Abstract presented to Parliament in 1833. But it is much to be regretted that their safe custody and preservation has not been secured by some stringent enactment. The old Scottish registers and the non-parochial English registers have under different[5] Acts of Parliament been securely deposited in the general registries of their respective countries:

---

[1] Report of Committee of the House of Commons on Parochial Registration, 1833. Evidence of Rev. J. E. Tyler and Mr. Burn.

[2] Evidence of Mrs. W. D. Cooper.

[3] Huntingdon Peerage, by R. N. Bell, 4to., 1820.

[4] Evidence of Mr. George Baker, June 25, 1833.

[5] *See* p. 11.

it is therefore monstrous that the parish registers of England, which are of more value than all the rest put together, should be the only registers in Great Britain for whose safety Parliament does not care to provide.

It never was intended that the existence of such valuable records should be left to depend on the fate of a single copy, and the provisions of the 70th Canon, that a transcript of the registers on parchment should be transmitted every year to the Bishop of the Diocese, were expressly devised as a security against loss negligence and fraud. If this ordinance had been properly observed, there would have been no difficulty in making up local deficiencies; but the duplicates are seldom forthcoming when they are wanted, and when Lewisham Church was burnt down on December 20, 1830, and the registers from 1550 were destroyed by the fire, it was found that the Bishop's registry contained transcripts of the registers of only 24 years out of the whole series of 280 years. There are literally thousands of parish registers of which the duplicates are missing, and the deplorable condition of the unsorted mass remaining in the diocesan registries has been described in a former[1] page. It must not, however, be supposed that this lamentable state of things has continued without any effort on the part of the Legislature to provide a remedy. On the contrary, the Act of 1812 empowered the Bishops to make a survey of the buildings in which their registers were kept, and they were invited to report to the Privy Council a scheme for remunerating their Registrars for the trouble of arranging and indexing the transcripts. But notwithstanding this enactment, not a single report has been ever sent in to the Council; no attempt was made to survey the registries; and their contents remain unarranged unindexed and unconsultable. It is one of the most provoking features in the case, that the value of these transcripts, when they do exist, has been abundantly proved in courts of law, for they have repeatedly supplied evidence that the parish registers have been tampered with. In the Angell case, an agricultural labourer laid claim to property valued at a million, and succeeded in getting a verdict; but the fraud was defeated, and a rule for a new trial was granted on discovering, when the register produced in court was compared with the Bishop's transcript, that the name of the person buried had been altered from Margaret Ange to Marriott Angell. In the Leigh peerage case also, a baptism which had been erased from the parish register of Wigan, was found in the Bishop's transcript at Chester, and decided the case against the claimant.

Another drawback to the utility of the transcripts is that

[1] *See* page 11.

there are no means of knowing what duplicates the Bishops' registries contain; and it would be a real addition to the materials of English history, if the Parish Register Abstract were supplemented by a Parliamentary Return of all the transcripts remaining in the different Bishops' registries, year by year and parish by parish; so that it could be seen at a glance from a comparison of the two Returns, how much of the series has been preserved, and how much has been irreparably lost. This Return might be prepared with advantage, whilst the different schemes for the safe custody of parish registers are under the consideration of Parliament; for no scheme will be complete and effectual, which does not include the Bishops' transcripts.

The necessity of some statutory provision to arrest the further destruction of this important branch of the national records has long been admitted by every one who has had occasion to consult them, but the interest of a wider circle was attracted to the subject of parish registers and their contents by Colonel Chester's edition of the registers of Westminster Abbey, which was published by the Harleian Society in 1876. These registers abound with illustrious names, which are honoured and familiar wherever the English language is spoken, and the editor worked out the history of every person mentioned with marvellous accuracy and minuteness. He had qualified himself for his task by many years of patient research, and his unrivalled collections from Wills marriage licences and other unpublished authorities enabled him to correct on almost every page statements hitherto accepted without challenge in standard books of reference. No registers could be found in England, which better deserved the labour bestowed on them, for the history of all those who were married christened and buried in the great Abbey traverses the whole field of English biography; and this book, which is a classic in its own line, brought home to the most careless reader, what a mass of historical materials lies hidden in the registers, which are daily perishing before our eyes almost without attempt to perpetuate their contents. One of the results of this stimulus to public opinion was the formation of a society for the purpose of printing *in extenso* as many of the more important registers, as the members' subscriptions would allow. The registers accordingly, of several London City parishes and of Canterbury Cathedral have been published in this Series; and being edited by competent antiquaries are highly appreciated by genealogists. But there are no less than 9000 parish registers in England, and the work done by a Society, which annually prints a single volume is scarcely worth taking into account in any scheme for dealing with the whole number. On the other hand, to print the whole mass *in extenso*, is practically out of the question on the ground of expense. A register must be carefully and accurately copied before it can be printed with any advantage ; and it must be acknowledged that a very small proportion of the whole number of registers has any interest whatever for the general public. It is hopeless therefore to expect that some 10000 volumes will ever be printed at the public expense for the purpose of making the shreds of information scattered through their pages more available for literary and antiquarian students.

This being the case, the simpler remedy has been suggested of treating as national records all registers and transcripts of earlier date than 1837, and of removing them to the Record Office and the custody of the Master of the Rolls. This suggestion was embodied in a Bill, entitled *The Parish Register Preservation Act* 1882, which was brought into the House of Commons on 19 April last by Mr. Borlase M.P. for East Cornwall ; and although the exigencies of public business prevented the subject being discussed during the late session, there is little doubt that a similar Bill with some modifications will sooner or later receive the sanction of Parliament. The Bill provides that every existing register of earlier date than 1 July 1837, (the day on which the Civil Registration Act came into operation) and also every transcript thereof remaining in any diocesan registry, shall after the passing of this Act be under the charge and control of the Master of the Rolls, and shall be removed by his warrant to the Record Office, where the public shall be at liberty to search them on payment of a fee of 20s. for every general search and of 1s. for every particular search. But in order that the present custodians may not be deprived of their customary fee for searches and extracts by the removal, they are to be permitted to retain in their custody, for a period of 20 years from the passing of the Act, the registers made in the interval between 1 January 1813, (the day on which Rose's Act came into operation) and 1 July 1837. It was hoped that this last provision would reconcile the parochial clergy to the transfer, as their search fees are almost entirely derived from registers of modern date ; and when the 20 years expired at which these later registers were to be transferred to the Record Office, there would still remain in the hands of each incumbent some 70 years of registers.

The compulsory transfer of parish registers to the Record Office would undoubtedly ensure their safe custody for the future, and would leave them accessible to a large body of students. But on the other hand it has been urged with much force, that their removal to London would be a great discouragement to local research, and that many county histories could never have been written, if the registers could not have been consulted in the districts, to which they relate. The necessity for taking some prompt action in the matter cannot be gainsaid, but objections which are put forward by antiquarian writers of established reputation cannot be lightly disregarded: and when we are gravely assured by their authors, that the publication of such books as Dr. Jessopp's *One Generation of a Norfolk House* and Sir John Maclean's *History of Trigg Minor* would have been indefinitely postponed, if the local registers had been removed to London; we are forced to consider whether some means could not be devised of better reconciling local and national claims.

The canon of 1603 required the register-books then in existence to be transcribed on parchment at the expense of the parish, and if Parliament now authorised a similar transcript to be made in every parish of existing registers of earlier date than 1837, the original books might all be removed to the Record Office, whilst the transcript would remain with the parish. For all local purposes the copy would be much more useful than the original, because comparatively few of the clergy have sufficient antiquarian skill to decipher the ancient registers, and to fix the dates of entries correctly. It is not that the old books are so badly written as to be illegible, but they are written in courthand, which is a different character from the Italian hand now in use. The legal year too until 1752 began on 25 March instead of on 1 January, so that all the entries before 25 March are attributed to what we should now reckon as the preceding year.

The parochial rate, which would have to be levied to defray the expenses of the transcript, could not be more than trifling in amount, and if it was left to the option of the parishioners to act as they pleased about raising it, they could not fairly complain of being deprived of the custody of registers, for the preservation of which they refused to make so small a sacrifice. It is submitted therefore, that it would be a convenient solution of the problem, if the enactment of removal to the Record Office included a proviso, authorising every parish which thought fit to incur the expense to make for its own use a copy of the registers, transferred to the Record Office which copy, being duly certified, should have all the force of the original for local purposes. With this suggestion I take leave of those simple annals—

> 'Where to be born and die
> Of rich and poor is all the history.'

My Index is abbreviated from an exhaustive index, which was compiled as a labour of love by Mr. Thomas Mason, the Librarian of Stirling's and Glasgow Library, Glasgow.

INDEX.

I

Spottiswoode & Co., Printers, New-street Square, London.

71 188 S   C   55 3

Lightning Source UK Ltd.
Milton Keynes UK
17 April 2010

152974UK00006B/21/A